THE LESS TRAVELED ROAD
AND THE BIBLE

THE
LESS TRAVELED
ROAD
and the Bible

A Scriptural Critique of the
Philosophy of M. Scott Peck

H. Wayne House
Richard Abanes

HORIZON BOOKS

Camp Hill, Pennsylvania

Horizon Books
3825 Hartzdale Drive
Camp Hill, PA 17011

ISBN: 0-88965-117-5
© 1995 by Horizon Books
All rights reserved
Printed in the United States of America

95 96 97 98 99   5 4 3 2 1

Cover photos by Duane Walker

Table of Contents

Publisher's Preface

This book has been coming for a while.

Like millions of others, I read *The Road Less Traveled* without too many adverse reactions. It was in reading *The People of the Lie* that I was first brought up short by M. Scott Peck's advocacy of a deliverance team that would include representatives of various religions.

Case studies—not just my own—show exactly the opposite. A still little-known apologetic to the uniqueness of Jesus Christ is that His name powerfully prevails over the spirit forces of other religions.

Richard Abanes' research, as always, is exhaustive and relentless, and if you are familiar with the Bible, his prose, early on, will have the alarm bells ringing.

In the second section, Dr. Wayne House, a respected evangelical theologian, has brought the light of the Scriptures to bear on Peck's ideas. The result is a memorable and powerful exposé.

As an occasional reader of M. Scott Peck, M.D., and until now one not too distressed by his ideas, I have been shocked by this material—shocked to find where Peck's errancy and inclusivism lead him and how far he departs from Christian orthodoxy. These capable authors stand ready to extend the same awakening to you.

K. Neill Foster, Ph.D.
Publisher

Introduction

According to a 1994 *Newsweek* poll, millions of Americans are looking for "spiritual meaning."[1] Some 58 percent of the country's adult population, in fact, "feel the need to experience spiritual growth."[2] A brief stop by any local newsstand will confirm the reliability of these statistics. Full-length feature stories bearing titles such as "In Search of the Sacred,"[3] "Traffic Jam on the Spiritual Highway"[4] and "Talking to God"[5] are now commonplace in national publications. Americans, it seems, are making a concerted effort to answer some age-old questions: What is the meaning of life? Why are we here? Where are we going?

Assisting today's truth-seekers in their search for spiritual fulfillment and emotional well-being are countless self-help gurus who feel personally motivated, sometimes even "divinely" inspired, to lend a helping hand. They feed their wisdom and guidance to the spiritually hungry in various ways: lectures, videos, workshops, weekend retreats and—of course—books.

As of December 1994, 25 percent of the titles on the *New York Times* bestseller list were "on spiritual subjects."[6] Among the most popular manuals on personal growth were those written by best-selling authors Marianne Williamson (*A Return to Love*), Thomas Moore (*Care of the Soul*), John Bradshaw (*Creating Love: The Next Great Stage of Growth*) and Joseph Girzone (*Never Alone: A Personal Way to God*). Interestingly, the "primary discipline underlying most of their books is psychology," not theology.[7]

Dennis M. Doyle, teacher of ecclesiology at the University of Dayton, correctly observes that these authors have all been influenced by "Carl Jung and/or the twelve step programs associated with Alcoholics Anonymous (AA)."[8] At the same time, however, their works "criticize traditional approaches to therapy that ignore a person's spiritual life, and several even proclaim a celestial marriage between psychology and spirituality."[9]

This "marriage" of therapy for both mind and soul is perhaps best exemplified in the works of Harvard-educated psychiatrist M. Scott Peck, whose 1978 book *The Road Less Traveled* initiated the entire psychology-spirituality movement. As of April 26, 1994, his landmark volume was still on the *New York Times* bestseller list—a full 600 weeks after first appearing there. For this accomplishment, Peck has won himself a place in the *Guinness Book of World Records*. He is arguably the most famous and influential of all the counseling gurus promising spiritual and emotional wholeness.

Subsequent to his original bestseller, Peck has written several more books that take readers further along his road of personal growth. This route, as his first book implies, is one that he believes is "less traveled" than other roads on which people have walked in their search for answers. This no doubt explains the subtitle he chose for his first book: *A New Psychology of Love, Traditional Values and Spiritual Growth*.

Christian author Warren Smith notes in a 1995 article for the *SCP Journal* that Peck single-handedly "helped to spark a spiritual revolution that is still going on today."[10] Peck's influence on the Christian church has been especially strong since his alleged conversion in 1980 to Christianity. Smith explains:

> His writings over the last decade or so have also caused Christians to reexamine their faith in light of his teachings. His books are often found in Christian bookstores. There is no question

that his writings and his endorsements of others have had a profound impact on the spiritual marketplace.[11]

M. Scott Peck has successfully built a highway of healing into the spiritual terrain of America. But is Peck's road to emotional and spiritual growth a safe one? Where does his road begin? How is it traversed? To what destination does it lead? Are his views and counsel compatible with the path on which Christians are instructed to walk as they seek to follow the teachings of Jesus Christ?

Part 1 of this book—entitled "Psychology Meets Spirituality"—begins answering these and other questions through a careful presentation of Peck's doctrinal beliefs, general philosophy of life and moral character. The section is not intended to be a refutation of Peck's worldview, but simply an explanation of it. Through Part 1, the reader will obtain an understanding of exactly who Peck is and what he believes.

Part 2—entitled "Theology Meets Dr. Peck"—takes Peck's teachings and compares them to Scripture. The validity of his claims regarding the best route to spiritual, mental and emotional wellness is also explored. Both sections not only provide a comprehensive look at M. Scott Peck, but also at his "less traveled road." For many readers, the sights along the way will prove most disturbing.

Endnotes

1. Kantrowitz, Barbara. "In Search of the Sacred," *Newsweek*, November 28, 1994, p. 52.

2. Kantrowitz, p. 54.

3. Kantrowitz, pp. 52–55.

4. Doyle, Dennis M. "Traffic Jam on the Spiritual Highway," *Commonweal*, September 9, 1994, pp. 18–22.

5. Woodward, Kenneth. "Talking to God," *Newsweek*, January 6, 1992, pp. 39–43.

6. Taylor, Eugene. "Desperately Seeking Spirituality," *Psychol-*

ogy Today, November/December 1994, p. 56.

7. Doyle, p. 18.

8. Doyle, p. 18.

9. Doyle, p. 18.

10. Smith, Warren. "M. Scott Peck: Community and the Cosmic Christ," *SCP Journal*, Volume 19:2/3 1995, p. 21.

11. Smith, p. 21.

Part 1

Psychology Meets Spirituality

Richard Abanes

CHAPTER 1

Discipline, Love, Religion and Grace

*Few writers have touched more lives than Dr. Peck,
and few messages have empowered more people.*
— *Oprah Winfrey*[1]

Born in 1936, Morgan Scott Peck grew up on New York City's Park Avenue in "a secular household with 'rugged individualist' parents who 'neither desired nor trusted intimacy.' "[2] Peck rejected his first name in favor of Scott because he disliked the nickname "Morgie" that had been given to him by his father,[3] a prominent attorney who eventually became a judge.[4]

Peck was sent away to begin his high school years at the renowned Phillips Exeter Academy boarding school in New England. He has been quoted as saying that he was "miserably unhappy."[5] The pressures for social conformity there were extreme, which prompted Peck to spend virtually all his energy vying for a place among the more popular students. He finally managed to make the "in" crowd during his third year, but hated it.

At the age of 15, during spring break vacation, Peck refused to return to the Academy.[6] The next school year found him repeating 11th grade at Friends Seminary, a Quaker prep school in Manhattan.[7] Here he took a world religions class that introduced him to the first spiritual belief system that he would embrace—Zen Buddhism.[8]

Peck remembers himself as a "freakishly religious kid," but not at all into Christianity, which he considered mere "gobbledygook."[9] His religious interests at that time centered around more mystical concepts, as evidenced by his early acceptance of Zen. He also admits that his alleged conversion to Christianity in 1980 came through mysticism: "I entered Christianity . . . through Christian mysticism. I was a mystic first before I was a Christian."[10]

Even before entering high school he wanted to be a writer.[11] This desire was encouraged by a woman named Carolyn Bryant, the mother of one of Peck's classmates. She was the head of Bryant and Bryant, "a leading publishing agency of the day."[12] Bryant had a profound effect on young Peck. To this day, he describes her as one of "the blessings" of his life.[13] Even though he was only 13 and she was 45, Peck and Bryant apparently had a deep and intimate relationship. "She and I kind of fell in love. . . . She became my Auntie Mame, plying me with caviar, cigarettes, and champagne. And I'm sure if I had asked for them, women."[14]

After leaving Friends Seminary, Peck attended Middlebury College but was expelled in 1956 for protesting against ROTC. The school went so far as to nullify all of his academic credits. Fortunately, Peck's father was on Harvard's alumni council and, after pulling a few strings, was able to get the prestigious institution to admit his son and restore the lost credits.[15]

Peck ended up graduating *magna cum laude* from Harvard in 1958 with a degree in social relations.[16] He then went into medicine in deference to his father's wishes, receiving his M.D. from Case Western Reserve University School of Medicine in 1963.[17]

During a Columbia University premed physics class he

met Lily Ho, a Chinese girl born and raised in Singapore.[18] They began dating, although both sets of parents objected to the interracial relationship. Lily's father—a Chinese Baptist minister—was distraught because of Peck's involvement with Buddhism.[19] Peck's mother and father were angered because their son was courting someone of Asian ancestry.[20]

Despite familial opposition, Scott and Lily married in December of 1959.[21] Peck's parents were so upset that they disinherited him. Eventually, however, tempers cooled and he was reinherited. In fact, Peck's father ended up paying his son's tuition and giving the newlyweds $100 a month until their first child was born nearly two years later.[22]

After graduating from medical school, Peck joined the military and, throughout nine and a half turbulent years of the Vietnam War, served as a U.S. Army psychiatrist in Okinawa and Washington, D.C.[23] It took only about two years of military service for Peck to realize that America's involvement in the war "was evil."[24] Rather than voice his protests in the streets as he had once done, he chose a more covert campaign. Peck reveals that from his post at the Surgeon General's office in Washington D.C., he "leaked information to [columnist] Jack Anderson's people"; specifically, government-related information Peck "considered to be scandals."[25]

Peck's attempts at changing the government from within failed, and in 1972 he resigned from his consulting psychiatry position, having obtained the rank of lieutenant colonel. Frustrated and disillusioned, he was forced to concede that one man alone could not cure "the ills of government."[26]

He then moved with Lily to rural New England where he began a private psychiatry practice in New Preston, Connecticut.[27] It was there, "in his eighteenth-century farmhouse on Bliss Road that he began *The Road Less Traveled*."[28]

Peck claims to have written the first draft in less than 20 months[29] and maintains that it was actually a "calling" placed on his life by God. To use his words, he was "divinely inspired" to write *The Road Less Traveled* and couldn't have done it "without God's help."[30] According to a 1992 article in *Life*, Peck feels all of his books have been produced in response to a divine calling. "For years, he wouldn't sign a two-book deal, not wanting to 'put the Holy Spirit under contract.' "[31]

Some might agree that Peck's books are "inspired," especially *The Road Less Traveled*. Thanks to a decade-long reign on *The New York Times* bestseller list, it has been called "the most popular book in history after the Bible."[32] Such popularity may be due in part to the fact that it offers easy-to-understand, broadly appealing ways to rid oneself of numerous debilitating emotions such as fear, confusion, anger, regret, loneliness, guilt and grief.

According to Peck, all of life's problems can be solved if one will only commit oneself to Peck's course of spiritual and mental growth. This course may be summarized in four words: discipline, love, religion and grace. To these issues we now turn.

Discipline

"Life is difficult."[33] This is the premise upon which *The Road Less Traveled* is built, and based upon the book's sales, few would argue that life is easy. Peck, however, believes that he has discovered how to overcome life's troubles. His first step toward dealing with life's dilemmas is "discipline," or what he calls "the basic set of tools we require to solve life's problems."[34] With total discipline, promises Peck, "we can solve all problems."[35]

Part and parcel of "discipline" is accepting the fact that problems are actually a blessing rather than a curse. They "call forth our courage and our wisdom; indeed, they create our courage and our wisdom." Peck believes it is "only because of problems that we grow mentally and spiritually."[36] Hence, we should all be thankful for our problems.

Peck observes that wise people "learn not to dread but

actually to welcome problems and actually to welcome the pain of problems."[37] Herein lies the biggest hindrance to growth—the avoidance of pain. Problems bring pain and people do not like pain. Consequently, people avoid problems in order to avoid their accompanying pain, which in turn causes something even worse—chronic mental illness.

> This tendency to avoid problems and the emotional suffering inherent in them is the primary basis of all human mental illness. Since most of us have this tendency . . . most of us are mentally ill to a greater or lesser degree, lacking complete mental health.[38]

Thus Peck asserts that one's first step to mental/spiritual growth is to eradicate all fear of suffering and to accept the pain brought on by problems. This is done by realizing that problems and pain are necessary and good because they produce learning and growth. Peck's discipline, or his basic set of problem-solving tools, are actually techniques of suffering, "by which we experience the pain of problems in such a way as to work them through and solve them successfully, learning and growing in the process."[39]

There are four "tools," or steps, that make up discipline: (1) delaying gratification; (2) acceptance of responsibility; (3) dedication to truth; and (4) balance. According to Peck, these tools are "not complex." Nor do they demand "extensive training." They are simple techniques "with which pain is confronted rather than avoided."[40] The end result will be personal growth.

Delaying Gratification

Delaying gratification is "a process of scheduling the pain and pleasure of life in such a way as to enhance the pleasure by meeting and experiencing the pain first and getting it over with."[41] In other words, when faced with two issues, one should deal with the painful one first, then enjoy the pleasurable one.

If someone's daily job consists of four tasks, and only one of them is enjoyable, then it is best for that person to finish the unenjoyable tasks first. Peck maintains that this technique can be very helpful.

First, additional time is given to problems when they are confronted early. He observes that many people "simply do not take the time necessary to solve many of life's intellectual, social or spiritual problems."[42]

Second, dealing quickly with a problem prevents that problem from getting worse. For instance, take the case of a salesman with a family of six who loses his job and, instead of immediately searching for new employment because he hates interviews, takes a three-week vacation. Suddenly, a number of bills are due and he still has no job. At that point, an even greater stress is placed on him to find work.

Delaying gratification is Peck's way of getting people to accept the fact that problems do not just go away. One's willingness to use this tool and face problems early is closely linked to another problem-solving technique—acceptance of responsibility.

Acceptance of Responsibility

"We cannot solve life's problems except by solving them."[43] According to Peck this obvious truth is "seemingly beyond the comprehension of much of the human race" because many people refuse to accept responsibility for a problem that is indeed theirs.[44] When faced with a problem, a significant step toward resolving it is to resolutely declare, "This is *my* problem and it's up to me to solve it."[45]

In psychotherapeutic language, those who do not accept enough responsibility for their own problems are said to have a character disorder. To these individuals, problems are always someone else's fault. A person may also go to the opposite extreme by accepting too much responsibility. This results in an everything-is-my-fault mentality. Such a person is classically termed a neurotic.

Peck comments, "neurotics make themselves miserable; those with character disorders make everyone else miserable."[46] His solution for both neurotics and those with character disorders is simple—"assume responsibility where appropriate."[47] Unfortunately, Peck never mentions how someone is to know *exactly* where accepting responsibility is appropriate. Instead he simply moves on to his third tool of discipline.

Dedication to Truth

Dedication to truth is the same thing as dedication to reality. It is an essential component of personal growth.

> The more clearly we see the reality of the world, the better equipped we are to deal with the world. The less clearly we see the reality of the world—the more our minds are befuddled by falsehood, misperceptions and illusions—the less able we will be to determine correct courses of action and make wise decisions.[48]

Peck likens our view of reality to a map with which we negotiate the terrain of life. The more accurate our map, the better we get along in life.[49] Of course, we are not born with maps. We have to make them throughout life. Unfortunately, says Peck, most of us have damaged maps because of lousy upbringings. Some, however, simply stop making their map because the process is either too boring or too difficult.

Our only hope, Peck declares, is to keep making our maps while staying open to constant revisions based on new information as it becomes available. The worst thing one can do is to get stuck in dogmatic thinking.

> We are daily bombarded with new information as to the nature of reality. If we are to incorporate this information, we must continually revise our maps, and sometimes . . . make very major revi-

sions. The process of making revisions ... is painful, sometimes excruciatingly painful.[50]

When it comes to poor map-making, pain avoidance is again targeted as the enemy. It is the "major source of many of the ills of mankind."[51] Avoiding pain, which is marked by a refusal to change, gets us locked into false perceptions based on erroneous maps.

> What happens when one has striven long and hard to develop a working view of the world, a seemingly useful, workable map, and then is confronted with new information suggesting that that view is wrong and the map needs to be largely redrawn? ... What we do more often than not, and usually unconsciously, is to ignore the new information. ... We may denounce the new information as false, dangerous, heretical, the work of the devil. We may actually crusade against it, and even attempt to manipulate the world so as to make it conform to our view of reality. Rather than try to change the map, an individual may try to destroy the new reality. Sadly, such a person may expend much more energy ultimately in defending an outmoded view of the world than would have been required to revise and correct it in the first place.[52]

The bottom line is that "we must always hold truth, as best we can determine it, to be more important, more vital to our self-interest, than our comfort."[53] Mental health "is an ongoing process of dedication to reality at all costs."[54]

Associated with having an openness to new information is dedication to self-examination and personal challenge: "The only way that we can be certain that our map of reality is valid is to expose it to the criticism and challenge of other map-makers."[55]

Peck believes that it is psychotherapy that presents one with the greatest opportunity for such self-examination and challenge. Through psychotherapy "we deliberately lay ourselves open to the deepest challenge from another human being, and even pay the other for the service of scrutiny and discernment."[56]

Entering psychotherapy, says Peck, "is an act of the greatest courage."[57] In fact, the level of courage needed to undergo psychotherapy demonstrates that patients "are basically much stronger and healthier than average."[58] He goes so far as to say that "most people who look like adults are actually just emotional children" and that "those who come to psychotherapy with genuine intent to grow are those *relative few* who are called out of immaturity, who are no longer willing to tolerate their own childishness. . . . *The rest of the population* [emphasis added] never manages to fully grow up. . . ."[59]

Such hard-core endorsements of psychotherapy are predictable. After all, Peck is a psychiatrist. However, he may be especially protective and complimentary of those needing psychotherapy because he himself entered psychotherapy at the age of 30 after reaching a psychological breaking point. In his 1993 book *Further Along the Road Less Traveled*, he writes about how he can still remember his shaking fingers "trembling their way through the Yellow Pages looking for a psychotherapist."[60] To those who would say that psychotherapy is a crutch, Peck offers a rebuttal.

> The use of psychotherapy is no more a crutch than the use of hammer and nails to build a house. It is possible to build a house without hammer and nails, but the process is generally not efficient or desirable. . . . Similarly, it is possible to achieve personal growth without employing psychotherapy, but often the task is unnecessarily tedious, lengthy and difficult.[61]

Balance

The final tool of discipline is "balance," which keeps discipline itself in check. It is characterized by an ability to negotiate "conflicting needs, goals, duties, responsibilities, directions, et cetera."[62] The essence of balance is "giving up."[63] For example, in order to control and use anger appropriately, one must first give up "the luxury of spontaneous anger or the safety of withheld anger."[64]

Balance often means giving up a long-held image of oneself as being emotionally and mentally healthy. By letting go of such an image, we are able to focus on those places within us that need to be changed. We must also be willing to give up old desires, hopes and dreams in favor of new things as we and the world around us change. In other words, balance equals flexibility.

These tools of discipline are difficult to practice, let alone master. What, then, gives someone the will to use such techniques? According to Peck, the motivation, strength and energy to put discipline into action comes from an actual force—love.[65] This leads us to the second major tenet of Peck's less traveled road.

Love

Peck defines love as the will to "extend one's self for the purpose of nurturing one's own or another's spiritual growth."[66] In this definition are five important points:[67]

1. Love is goal-oriented. Its end is spiritual growth.
2. Love is a circular process. By loving others, we extend ourselves, which in turn produces growth in us.
3. Love for others includes self-love.
4. Love involves effort because it takes work to extend one's limits.
5. Love does not always involve desire. It is often an action resulting from a conscious choice of will.

An interesting aspect of Peck's view of love involves his belief that " 'falling in love' is a sort of illusion which in no way constitutes real love."[68] In some respects, writes Peck, "the act of falling in love is an act of regression. The experience of merging with the loved one has in it echoes from the time when we were merged with our mothers in infancy."[69]

To Peck, "falling in love" is nothing more than a temporary collapse of ego boundaries (that inner recognition of where our psyche stops and the outside world begins, which is something absent in babies), infused with sexuality. He suspects that the experience is nothing more than genetics.

> [T]he sexual specificity of the phenomenon [of falling in love] leads me to suspect that it is a genetically determined instinctual component of mating behavior . . . a stereotypic response of human beings to a configuration of internal sexual drives and external sexual stimuli, which serves to increase the probability of sexual pairing and bonding so as to enhance the survival of the species. Or to put it in another, rather crass way, falling in love is a trick that our genes pull on our otherwise perceptive mind to hoodwink or trap us into marriage. . . . [W]ithout this trick, this illusory and inevitably temporary (it would not be practical were it not temporary) regression to infantile merging . . . many of us who are happily or unhappily married today would have retreated in wholehearted terror from the realism of the marriage vows.[70]

Peck does not mean to say that this biological reaction is wholly worthless. Falling in love often leads one into a relationship which, once it is void of feelings, may provide an atmosphere where real love—as Peck defines it—can blossom. Only when emotions are absent can "true love" be demonstrated.

> [R]eal love often occurs in a context in which the feeling of love is lacking. . . . Assuming the reality of the definition of love with which we started, the experience of "falling in love" is not real love. . . .[71]

For those who fear they might not be able to show "real love" in the absence of feelings, Peck offers a word of assurance: "[G]enuine love for a relatively few individuals is all that is within our power."[72] In other words, we only need to love a few people, since that is all that any human being is capable of doing.

Peck further reveals that some people will be unable to respond to our love. In such instances, rather than getting discouraged, it is simply best not to waste our time with them.

> To attempt to love someone who cannot benefit from your love with spiritual growth is to waste your energy, to cast your seed upon arid ground. . . . [T]hose who are capable of genuine love know that their loving must be focused as productively as possible through self-discipline.[73]

The entire thesis of *The Road Less Traveled* is that "lasting enlightenment or true spiritual growth can be achieved only through the persistent exercise of real love."[74] With this statement, readers are given the urgency of finding someone to love—by loving others, we are actually accelerating our own growth. Herein is the motivation for loving: selfishness. The well-being of another is not why we should love.

> The more I love, the longer I love, the larger I become. Genuine love is self-replenishing. The more I nurture the spiritual growth of others, the more my own spiritual growth is nurtured. I am a totally selfish human being. *I never do something*

for somebody else but that I do it for myself. And as I
grow through love, so grows my joy, ever more
present, ever more constant [emphasis added].[75]

Peck further explains that we never really do *anything* for
someone else. There is no such thing as love demonstrated
through sacrificial acts. Even if we think we are doing a
deed for someone else, our true motivation is always self.
Thinking that one's sacrificial acts are loving amounts to
little more than masochism (deriving pleasure from one's
own suffering or pain).

> The issue of masochism highlights still another
> very major misconception about love—that it is
> self-sacrificing. . . . Whenever we think of our-
> selves as doing something *for* someone else, we
> are in some way denying our own responsibil-
> ity. Whatever we do is done because we choose
> to do it, and we make that choice because it is
> the one that satisfies us the most. Whatever we
> do for someone else we do because it fulfills a
> need we have.[76]

Real love, Peck asserts, is actually just as selfish as nonlove. In fact, the selfishness or unselfishness of an act is not
what makes it loving or unloving. The *aim* of the action is
what identifies something as loving: "In the case of genuine love the aim is always spiritual growth. In the case of
nonlove the aim is always something else."[77]

But Peck realizes that his definition of love begs some
questions: Where does love itself, and all those emotions
related to it, actually come from? What of the love that an
artist has for his works? Why do we often shed tears when
confronted by love?

Peck responds: "The people who know the most about
such things are those among the religious who are students
of Mystery. It is to them and to the subject of religion that

we must turn if we are to obtain even glimmerings of insight into these matters."[78] Readers are thus shuttled into a discussion of the relationship between religion and the growth process.

Religion

Part 3 of *The Road Less Traveled* tells us that throughout humanity is "an extraordinary variability in the breadth and sophistication of our understanding of what life is all about" and that this understanding "is our religion."[79] Since everyone has some kind of worldview, then everyone also has some kind of religion.

Peck contends that to some extent, "the religion of most adults is a product of transference."[80] In psychotherapy, "transference" refers to what occurs when a "set of ways of perceiving and responding to the world which is developed in childhood and which is usually entirely appropriate to the childhood environment . . . is *inappropriately* transferred into the adult environment."[81]

What this means is that most adults need to revise, or update, their "map" of reality as new knowledge about the cosmos becomes available to them. This would include their religious concepts. Peck bluntly states that we "must rebel against and reject the religion of our parents, for inevitably their worldview will be narrower than that of which we are capable."[82] To illustrate his point, he pulls from personal experiences with patients.

> Many patients who have already taken this beginning say to me: "I'm not religious. I don't go to church. I no longer believe much of what the church and my parents told me. I don't have my parents' faith. I guess I'm not very spiritual." It often comes as a shock to them when I question the reality of their assumption that they are not spiritual beings. "You have a religion," I may

say, "a rather profound one. You worship the truth. . . . I suspect the reality is that you have spiritually evolved beyond your parents, that your spirituality is greater by a quantum leap than theirs, which is insufficient to provide them with even the courage to question."[83]

Peck tells us that "psychotherapists must spend enormous amounts of time and effort in the struggle to liberate their patients' minds from outmoded religious ideas and concepts that are clearly destructive."[84] At the same time, however, he believes psychotherapy has gone too far by completely eradicating all concepts of God. They have committed the proverbial error of "throwing out the baby with the bath water."[85]

Belief in God per se—whatever one's concept of God may be—is not the problem, asserts Peck. The real problem is dogmatism.[86] To cure this human ill, one must be ready to "give up" old religious ideas and adopt a more tolerant attitude toward new concepts. It must begin by "distrusting what we already believe . . . by deliberately challenging the validity of what we have previously been taught and hold dear."[87]

One should not go too far, however, because "there is reason to believe that behind spurious notions and false concepts of God there lies a reality that is God."[88] With this statement, Peck segues into the subject of grace, which directly relates to his view of God.

Grace

To Peck, "an understanding of the phenomenon of grace is essential to complete understanding of the process of growth in human beings."[89] He begins explaining his concept of grace by introducing various phenomena he refers to as miracles: (1) health, (2) unconscious and (3) serendipity/synchronicity.

The Miracle of Health

One of Peck's most interesting assertions is that psychiatric patients, despite their need for therapy, "are amazingly healthy mentally."[90] What Peck means is that although a high degree of mental illness is caused by severe trauma during childhood (e.g., physical abuse, sexual molestation, etc.), one seldom sees a patient who is "not basically healthier mentally than their parents."[91]

It is often known why people become mentally ill, but what is not known—and what is the most fascinating to Peck—is "why people survive the traumas of their lives as well as they do."[92] What is even more puzzling to Peck is why some survive better than others.

Peck poses similar questions regarding physical health, and observes that "we have almost no knowledge of how resistance works."[93] Why do some people experience heart attacks, strokes, cancer, peptic ulcers, etc., while others do not? "An increasing number of thinkers," Peck asserts, "are beginning to suggest that almost all disorders are psychosomatic—that the psyche is somehow involved in the causation of the various failures that occur in the resistance system."[94]

But it is not our diseases that Peck is interested in; it is our health. He is baffled as to why our resistance system works as well as it does given all the pollutants, germs and viruses plaguing the planet.

> In the ordinary course of things we should be eaten alive by bacteria, consumed by cancer, clogged up by fats and clots, eroded by acids. It is hardly remarkable that we sicken and die; what is truly remarkable is that we don't usually sicken very often and we don't die very quickly.[95]

Peck's explanation for both mental and physical health is unquestionably mystical: "[T]here is a force, the mechanics of which we do not fully understand, that seems to operate routinely in most people to protect and to foster their mental [and physical] health even under the most adverse conditions."[96]

The frequency of accidents in a particular person's life is also mentioned. Why do some people seem unusually accident-prone while others live virtually accident-free? How can an individual emerge unharmed from an automobile accident in which her car was demolished beyond recognition while someone else is killed in a much less severe collision?

Peck continues: "Could it be that most of us do lead 'charmed lives'? Could it really be that the line in the song is true: 'Tis grace hath brought me safe thus far'?"[97] Before answering these questions, Peck takes the reader on a detour to examine yet another "miracle"—the unconscious mind.

The Miracle of the Unconscious

Psychotherapy rests largely upon the presupposition that our minds can be divided into basically two parts: the conscious and the unconscious. In the unconscious mind—which according to Peck comprises 95 percent or more of our total mind—there allegedly exists "riches beyond imagination."[98] It is a veritable storehouse of knowledge about ourselves. It alone "knows who we really are."[99]

Unfortunately, the conscious (waking) part of our mind cannot communicate with the unconscious part. So it is up to the unconscious to somehow establish a message link. One way it supposedly does this is through dreams.[100] A majority of psychotherapists, including Peck, feel that dreams display what a person truly thinks and feels. This is why dream interpretation is "a significant part" of psychotherapy.[101]

Another way the unconscious supposedly attempts to communicate with the conscious is through "'idle thoughts,' or even fragments of thoughts."[102] This is why psychotherapy patients are often instructed to say "*whatever* comes into their mind no matter how silly or insignificant it may initially seem [emphasis in original]."[103]

The unconscious is often looked at by psychotherapists as

an entirely separate entity that actually wants to work with and assist us (our conscious self).[104] The unconscious mind is so separate from the conscious mind that the former is able to gather insights not only into the self, but also into others and the surrounding world.[105] Legendary Swiss psychiatrist and psychologist Carl Jung (1875–1961) referred to this knowledge as "The Wisdom of the Unconscious."

Jung's concept is shared by Peck.[106] As a result, he argues that a "major and essential task in the process of one's spiritual development is the continuous work of bringing one's conscious self-concept into progressively greater congruence with reality,"[107] which is perceived much better by the unconscious. In other words, "our unconscious is wiser than we are about everything."[108] Our job is to learn from it.

Another Jungian concept accepted by Peck is that of a "collective unconscious," which theorizes that "we inherit the wisdom of the experience of our ancestors without ourselves having the personal experience."[109] This collective unconscious is said to be "the storehouse of the accumulated memories and forms of behavior that date back to the dawn of the human species."[110] Peck explains:

> The great psychiatrist Carl Jung posited a phenomenon he called "the collective unconscious." This he described as a part of the individual mind that is not conscious but that is somehow shared with the same part of the minds of others. In his psychology this collective unconscious is a kind of semi-intellectual garden of delights that is owned by humanity in common, which every human being is free to visit in his dreams or roam in her deepest interior life.[111]

It is here that the importance of myths and legends come into play. According to Jung, the myths and legends of various cultures include archetypes (i.e., original truths or concepts). These archetypes, stored in the collective unconscious, are said to emerge as symbols time and time again through the stories passed on from generation to generation. As we shall later see, this is an extremely important part of Peck's views about God.

Peck goes even further in his speculations about the unconscious by linking this allegedly hidden part of our minds to "psychic phenomena," which he maintains "are clearly related to the operation of the unconscious mind."[112] In support of such phenomena, Peck cites his third "miracle"—serendipity/synchronicity.

The Miracle of Serendipity/Synchronicity

The concept of synchronicity, like the concept of the "wisdom" of the unconscious, was proposed by psychoanalyst Carl Jung.[113] Terence Hines, an assistant professor of psychology at Pace University, explains in his 1988 book *Pseudoscience and the Paranormal* that according to synchronicity there is no such thing as a coincidence. All apparent coincidences are actually meaningful events.[114] He gives an illustration.

> If I bought a blue frock and, by mistake, the shop delivered a black one on the day one of my near relatives died, this would be a meaningful coincidence. The two events are not causally related, but they are connected by the symbolic meaning that our society gives to the color black.[115]

According to Jung, such coincidences, although unrelated by cause and effect, do not occur at random. They have meaning and are orchestrated.[116] Jung pointed out that such events tend to occur "at psychologically important times in an individual's life,"[117] which to him proved the theory. Synchronicity is explained well in *The Road Less Traveled.*

> The fact that highly implausible events, for which no cause can be determined within the

framework of known natural law, occur with implausible frequency has come to be known as synchronicity.[118]

As an example of this phenomenon, Peck mentions a personal experience wherein he and a friend had the same dream two days apart. He also relates the following story obtained from a patient.

> . . . I decided to drive home by the route around the lake. . . . [T]he road around the lake has a great many blind curves. I was approaching perhaps the tenth of these curves when the thought suddenly occurred to me that a car could be racing around the corner far into my side of the road. Without any more thought than that, I vigorously braked my car and came to a dead stop. No sooner had I done this than a car did indeed come barreling around the curve with its wheels six feet across the yellow line and barely missed me even though I was standing still on my side of the road. Had I not stopped, it is inevitable that we would have collided at the curve. I have no idea what made me decide to stop. . . . It makes me wonder whether there really isn't something to ESP [extrasensory perception] and things like that.[119]

Peck uses synchronicity to bring up what he refers to as "the phenomenon of serendipity." Webster's Dictionary defines this phenomenon as "the gift of finding valuable or agreeable things not sought for."[120] Examples of serendipity would be: (1) discovering a $20 bill in a street drain (2) needing to find information on a particular subject and coincidentally receiving a call from a friend who is giving away books containing the needed material or (3) hitting the save button on a computer just before a power surge hits that would have erased the document had the save button not been pressed.

Such episodes are commonly referred to as "strokes of luck." But the concept of luck is rejected by Peck. He believes "that our growth as human beings is being assisted by a force other than our conscious will."[121] That force—manifested as serendipity/synchronicity, health and knowledge imparted to the unconscious mind—is grace.

> [T]hese phenomena are part of or manifestations of a single phenomenon: a powerful force originating outside of human consciousness which nurtures the spiritual growth of human beings. . . . [T]his force has been consistently recognized by the religious, who have applied to it the name of grace. And have sung its praise. "Amazing grace, how sweet the sound."[122]

According to Peck, the source of grace is none other than God. Exactly what does Peck mean by God? The answer to this question may surprise many people, especially Christians.

The God Within

On page 261 of *The Road Less Traveled*, Peck notes that for centuries grace has been attributed in some way to an entity called "God." Believing that grace originates from "God" is certainly acceptable to Peck. In fact, he believes that the existence of grace "is *prima facie* evidence not only of the reality of God but also of the reality that God's will is devoted to the growth of the individual human spirit."[123]

The idea that God exists as an individual entity has also been passed down to us through the centuries. According to Peck, this is nothing but a by-product of man's "profound tendency to conceptualize in terms of discrete entities."[124]

> We perceive the world composed of such entities: ships, shoes and sealing wax. . . . It is either this or that, but it cannot be both. Ships are ships and not shoes. I am I and you are you. The I-entity is my identity and the you-entity is your identity. . . . Our tendency to entity-thinking compels us to want to locate things, *even such things as God* [emphasis added].[125]

Peck reveals that he does not "think of the individual as a true entity at all," but conceives "of the boundaries of the individual as being marked by a most permeable membrane—a fence, if you will, instead of a wall; a fence through which, under which and over which other 'entities' may climb, crawl or flow."[126]

"Just as our conscious mind is continually partially permeable to our unconscious," he continues, "so is our unconscious permeable to the 'mind' without, the 'mind' that permeates us yet is not us as entities."[127]

Peck is echoing a concept found in Hinduism and Buddhism, namely, that all reality is oneness and that what we perceive to be individuality is an illusion. This illusion in Eastern thought is termed "maya." Such a view is first articulated only in passing on page 96 of *The Road Less Traveled*, but by page 262 it is presented as a reality.

> As we have previously noted, Hindu and Buddhist thinkers believe our perception of discrete entities to be illusion, or maya, and modern physicists, concerned with relativity, wave-particle phenomena, electromagnetism, et cetera, are becoming increasingly aware of the limitations of our conceptual approach in terms of entities.[128]

The above concept is a major tenet of the New Age movement, as New Age spokesperson David Spangler demonstrates when he writes, "Oneness is a key concept. In a spiritual sense, the world has always been one. . . . This oneness has expressed itself in apparent diversity and separation. . . . Oneness is the only reality and diversity is its apparent manifestation."[129]

Christian author Elliot Miller explains this belief in his insightful work *A Crash Course on the New Age Movement*.

> *All* New Agers believe that "all is one"—everything that exists consists of one and the same essence or reality. A second assumption is that this Ultimate Reality is neither dead matter nor unconscious energy. It is Being, Awareness, and Bliss (which is to say, a Hindu conception of God as an impersonal, infinite consciousness and force). The first assumptions imply two more: all that is, is God (which is *pantheism*); and man, a part of "all that is," is likewise divine. But how do New Agers answer the inescapable fact that most people do not at all *feel* one with God? . . . New Agers explain that man is separated from God *only* in his own consciousness. He is the victim of a *false* sense of separate identity which blinds him to his essential unity with God, and this is the cause of all his problems.[130]

Like all New Agers, Peck embraces the belief that realization of our oneness with God—or our own godhood—is essential to spiritual growth and freedom from problems. Attaining godhood is really the only reason we exist. Realization of our divinity is also the whole purpose behind evolution, which is another "miracle" to Peck: "I believe we can benefit from considering yet another miracle: the growth process of all life itself, to which we have given the name evolution."[131]

After establishing as fact the idea that all is one and that evolution is a reality by which humans change both physically and spiritually, Peck boldly and forcefully declares what he believes to be our ultimate goal.

> We are growing toward godhood. God is the goal of evolution. It is God who is the source of the evolutionary force and God who is the destination. That is what we mean when we say that He is the Alpha and the Omega, the beginning and the end. . . . It is one thing to believe in a nice old God who will take good care of us from a lofty position of power which we ourselves could never begin to attain. It is quite another to believe in a God who has it in mind for us precisely that we should attain His position, His power, His wisdom, His identity. . . . But we do not want this obligation. . . . As long as we can believe that godhood is an impossible attainment for ourselves, we don't have to worry about our spiritual growth. . . . If God's in His heaven and we're down here . . . we can let Him have all the responsibility for evolution and the directorship of the universe. . . . [But] as soon as we believe it is possible for man to become God, we can never really rest for long. . . . We must constantly push ourselves to greater and greater wisdom. . . . It is no wonder that the belief in the possibility of Godhead [sic] is repugnant.[132]

Peck is not saying here that we are not already "God." He is simply stating that most people either do not know they are God, or avoid conscious acceptance of their divinity because of fear. He clearly holds that all of us are already divine; more specifically, it is our unconscious that is divine.

> If you want to know the closest place to look for grace, it is within yourself. If you desire wisdom greater than your own, you can find it inside

you. What this suggests is that the interface between God and man is at least in part the interface between our unconscious and our conscious. To put it plainly, our unconscious is God. God within us. We were part of God all the time. God has been with us all along, is now, and always will be. . . . If the reader is horrified by the notion that our unconscious is God, he or she should recall that it is hardly a heretical concept, being in essence the same as the Christian concept of the Holy Ghost or Holy Spirit which resides in us all.[133]

Peck actually believes that Jung's "collective unconscious" is God, while each personal "consciousness" is man as an illusory individual self.[134] How does this all fit in with psychological wellness? Peck says that all mental disorders reside in the conscious mind because our conscious self continually "resists our unconscious wisdom,"[135] which contains the knowledge of our godhood.

In other words, "mental illness occurs when the conscious will of the individual deviates substantially from the will of God, *which is the individual's own unconscious will* [emphasis added]."[136] With this statement, Peck is able to bring his readers to what he calls "the point of it all":

Since the unconscious is God all along, we may further define the goal of spiritual growth to be the attainment of godhood by the conscious self. It is for the individual to become totally, wholly God. . . . The point is to become God while preserving consciousness. If the bud of consciousness that grows from the rhizome [root-like stem] of the unconscious God can become itself God, then God will have assumed a new life form.[137]

31

Here Peck diverges from classic Eastern thought, which teaches a sort of blissful *unconscious* merging with the divine. In this state of existence, termed *nirvana*, all individuality is lost.

Peck, on the other hand, is encouraging nothing less than a concious reunion with "God"; a development of "a mature, conscious ego which then can become the ego of God."[138] "This is the meaning of our individual existence," Peck finally reveals. "We are born that we might become, as a conscious individual, a new life form of God."[139]

Two years after writing these words, Peck purportedly became a Christian (1980). He announced his "conversion" unapologetically in his second book, *People of the Lie: The Hope for Healing Human Evil*, which deals primarily with the nature of evil and sin. In this volume, he also acknowledges the reality of Satan and repeatedly points to Jesus Christ as the answer for humanity.

But when Peck speaks of "Jesus," "evil," "Satan" and other Christian concepts, what exactly does he mean? In the next chapter we shall take a closer look at Peck's brand of Christianity. It is hardly conventional. Ironically, his second bestseller begins with a rather ominous warning that is perhaps more insightful than Peck intended it to be. The opening page reads, "This is a dangerous book."[140]

Endnotes

1. "Oprah Winfrey Show," on KABC (December 8, 1993), written transcript as quoted in "M. Scott Peck: Community and the Cosmic Christ" by Warren Smith, *SCP Journal*, 19:2/3, p. 21.

2. Dart, John. "Spiritual-Growth Evangelism: Path to World Peace?," *Los Angeles Times*, June 17, 1987, p. 1.

3. Dart, p.1.

4. Scheinin, Richard. "Author M. Scott Peck Challenges Our Notions of Love and Spiritual Growth," *San Jose Mercury News*, February 19, 1991, p. 8D; cf. "M. Scott Peck" by Diane Connors, *Omni*, October 1988, p. 126.

5. Miller, Russell. "The Road Warrior," *Life*, December 1992, p. 74.

6. Peck, M. Scott. *The Different Drum* (New York: Simon & Schuster, 1987), p. 29.

7. Miller, p. 74.

8. Connors, p. 126; cf. Scheinin, p. 8D and "Playboy Interview: M. Scott Peck" by David Sheff, *Playboy*, March 1992, p. 58.

9. Connors, p. 129.

10. Dart, p. 4.

11. Connors, p. 128.

12. Connors, p. 128.

13. Connors, p. 128.

14. Connors, p. 128.

15. Sheff, p. 59; cf. Connors, p. 131.

16. Dart, p. 1; cf. Connors, p. 126.

17. Connors, p. 126; cf. Dart, p. 1.

18. Connors, pp. 126, 128; cf. Sheff, p. 44.

19. Connors, p. 126.

20. Sheff, p. 59.

21. Connors, p. 128.

22. Connors, p. 128.

23. Connors, p. 128; cf. Sheff, p. 44.

24. Sheff, p. 59.

25. Sheff, p. 60.

26. Dart, p. 1.

27. Connors, p. 126; cf. Dart, p. 1 and Miller, p. 74.

28. Connors, p. 126.

29. Connors, p. 130.

30. "Oprah Winfrey Show" written transcript as quoted in Smith, p. 22.

31. Miller, p. 79; cf. Sheff, pp. 44, 46.

32. Scheinin, p. 1D.

33. Peck, M. Scott. *The Road Less Traveled* (New York: Simon & Schuster, 1978), p. 15.

34. Peck, *The Road*, p. 15.

35. Peck, *The Road*, p. 16.

36. Peck, *The Road*, p. 16.

37. Peck, *The Road*, p. 16.

38. Peck, *The Road*, pp. 16–17.

39. Peck, *The Road*, pp. 17–18.

40. Peck, *The Road*, p. 18.

41. Peck, *The Road*, p. 19.

42. Peck, *The Road*, p. 28.

43. Peck, *The Road*, p. 32.

44. Peck, *The Road*, p. 32.

45. Peck, *The Road*, p. 32.

46. Peck, *The Road*, p. 38.

47. Peck, *The Road*, p. 36.

48. Peck, *The Road*, p. 44.

49. Peck, *The Road*, p. 44.

50. Peck, *The Road*, p. 45.

51. Peck, *The Road*, p. 45.

52. Peck, *The Road*, pp. 45–46.

53. Peck, *The Road*, p. 50.

54. Peck, *The Road*, p. 50.

55. Peck, *The Road*, p. 52.

56. Peck, *The Road*, p. 53.

57. Peck, *The Road*, p. 53.

58. Peck, *The Road*, p. 54.

59. Peck, M. Scott. *Further Along the Road Less Traveled* (New York: Simon & Schuster, 1993), p. 20.

60. Peck, *Further*, p. 93.

61. Peck, *The Road*, p. 57.

62. Peck, *The Road*, p. 66.

63. Peck, *The Road*, p. 66.

64. Peck, *The Road*, p. 67.

65. Peck, *The Road*, p. 81.

66. Peck, *The Road*, p. 81.

67. Peck, *The Road*, pp. 82–83.

68. Peck, *The Road*, p. 94.

69. Peck, *The Road*, p. 87.

70. Peck, *The Road*, p. 90.

71. Peck, *The Road*, p. 88.

72. Peck, *The Road*, pp. 157–58.

73. Peck, *The Road*, p. 158.

74. Peck, *The Road*, p. 97.

75. Peck, *The Road*, p. 160.

76. Peck, *The Road*, pp. 115–116.

77. Peck, *The Road*, p. 116.

78. Peck, *The Road*, pp. 181-182.

79. Peck, *The Road,* p. 185.
80. Peck, *The Road,* p. 192.
81. Peck, *The Road,* p. 46.
82. Peck, *The Road,* p. 194.
83. Peck, *The Road,* pp. 195–196.
84. Peck, *The Road,* pp. 207–208.
85. Peck, *The Road,* p. 224.
86. Peck, *The Road,* p. 222.
87. Peck, *The Road,* p. 194.
88. Peck, *The Road,* p. 223.
89. Peck, *The Road,* p. 182.
90. Peck, *The Road,* p. 236.
91. Peck, *The Road,* p. 237.
92. Peck, *The Road,* p. 237.
93. Peck, *The Road,* p. 239.
94. Peck, *The Road,* p. 239.
95. Peck, *The Road,* p. 239.
96. Peck, *The Road,* pp. 237–238; cf. p. 239.
97. Peck, *The Road,* p. 241.
98. Peck, *The Road,* p. 243.
99. Peck, *The Road,* p. 251.
100. Peck, *The Road,* p. 243.
101. Peck, *The Road,* p. 244.
102. Peck, *The Road,* p. 245.
103. Peck, *The Road,* p. 245.
104. Peck, *The Road,* p. 244.
105. Peck, *The Road,* p. 245.
106. Peck, *The Road,* p. 247.
107. Peck, *The Road,* p. 251.
108. Peck, *The Road,* p. 251.
109. Peck, *The Road,* p. 252.
110. Hines, Terence. *Pseudoscience and the Paranormal* (Buffalo, NY: Prometheus Books, 1988), p. 138.
111. Peck, M. Scott. *A World Waiting to Be Born* (New York: Bantam, 1993), p.361.
112. Peck, *The Road,* p. 253.
113. Hines, p. 105.
114. Hines, p. 105.
115. Hines, p. 138.
116. Hines, p. 138.

117. Hines, p. 138.

118. Peck, *The Road*, p. 254.

119. Peck, *The Road*, pp. 255–256.

120. Peck, *The Road*, p. 257.

121. Peck, *The Road*, p. 263.

122. Peck, *The Road*, p. 260.

123. Peck, *The Road*, p. 311.

124. Peck, *The Road*, p. 261.

125. Peck, *The Road*, pp. 261–262.

126. Peck, *The Road*, p. 262.

127. Peck, *The Road*, p. 262.

128. Peck, *The Road*, p. 262.

129. Spangler, David. *Revelation: The Birth of a New Age* (San Francisco: The Rainbow Bridge, 1976), pp. 191, 194.

130. Miller, Eliot. *A Crash Course on the New Age Movement* (Grand Rapids, MI: Baker Book House, 1989), p. 17.

131. Peck, *The Road*, p. 263.

132. Peck, *The Road*, pp. 270–271.

133. Peck, *The Road*, p. 281.

134. Peck, *The Road*, p. 282.

135. Peck, *The Road*, p. 282.

136. Peck, *The Road*, p. 282.

137. Peck, *The Road*, p. 283.

138. Peck, *The Road*, p. 283.

139. Peck, *The Road*, p. 283.

140. M. Scott Peck, *People of the Lie* (New York: Simon & Schuster, 1983), p. 9.

CHAPTER 2

The Essence of Evil

Enthralling, frustrating, controversial, paradoxical, revolutionary—People of the Lie *may well be one of the most significant new works in recent memory.*
—Contemporary Christian Magazine[1]

When *People of the Lie* first hit the bookstores, a number of Peck's fans were aghast. Their beloved secular psychiatrist had become a "Christian." Early in the book, he writes a thoroughly evangelical-sounding testimony.

> After many years of vague identification with Buddhist and Islamic mysticism, I ultimately made a firm Christian commitment—signified by my nondenominational baptism on the ninth of March 1980, at the age of forty-three—long after I had begun working on this book. . . . My commitment to Christianity is the most important thing in my life and is, I hope, pervasive and total.[2]

The Christian church—a segment of the book-buying market previously untapped by psychiatrists—welcomed

M. Scott Peck. Subsequently, "Scotty" was ushered from church to church as a born-again believer while Christian publications printed personal interviews with him and favorably reviewed his works. Consider the following endorsement from a 1985 *Christianity Today* article:

> *People of the Lie* is a remarkable book and well worth your time. . . . For pastors it provides some cracker-jack sermon illustrations. . . . More important, the book is invaluable for alerting the pastoral counselor to the dynamics of evil on an interpersonal level. . . . Peck's book has come along at a propitious time. It deserves a critical reading by evangelicals, but also a wide reading.[3]

Even before the release of *People of the Lie*, Peck had announced his "conversion" and, as a result, was beginning to garner support from Christians. A July 1981 issue of *News from Faith at Work* carried an interview with Peck in which he stated, "Jesus gently overtook me. . . . I'm a Christian and I didn't bring myself to it."[4] The article concludes with a supportive word from the Christian interviewer: "When you read *The Road Less Traveled*, which I hope you will, you will know from where Scott Peck's certainty about Grace derives."[5]

Peck's greatest popularity soon shifted from New York and Los Angeles to the Bible Belt.[6] By 1985 *The Road Less Traveled* and *People of the Lie* were sixth and seventh on *Eternity* magazine's Book of the Year list.[7] This relationship between Peck and the Christian community remains strong to this day.

Peck says he became a Christian after finding himself "thirsting for a less abstract and a more flesh-and-blood kind of God."[8] He allegedly discovered Christianity's more tangible deity thanks to a spiritual quest initiated by the comments of book reviewers who, after reading *The Road*

Less Traveled, mistakenly thought Peck was already a born-again believer.

> When the reviews of *The Road* started coming in and one said, "His voice is predominantly Christian," Peck's startled response was, "Wow! Have I become a Christian?" He read the New Testament then seriously for the first time and "Jesus became incredibly real to me," he recalls.[9]

Peck subsequently made his way to an Episcopal convent on the Hudson River near his home in Connecticut and chose one of the sisters residing there to be his spiritual teacher. The search for spiritual fulfillment culminated in his baptism at the hands of a visiting Methodist minister.[10]

Even as Peck was supposedly embracing Christianity, he "found that he had to address the subject of evil."[11] Thus was born his second book *People of the Lie. Christianity Today* described it as a work "loaded with the fascinating and chilling stories" of patients who had "struggled with evil people or who were themselves evil."[12]

Peck's concept of evil is dependent upon his beliefs about the origin and nature of a closely related issue—sin. As previously noted, Peck holds that true spiritual growth is marked by conscious recognition of our inherent godhood, the ultimate goal of that realization being transformation into a new life form of God. Any impediments to achieving this ultimate spiritual goal are what Peck considers sins.

But what *exactly* does it mean to commit a "sin"? Peck maintains that sinning is "most broadly defined as 'missing the mark.' This means that we sin every time we fail to hit the bull's-eye. Sin is nothing more and nothing less than a failure to be continually perfect."[13]

It is an inescapable fact, says Peck, that "we are all sinners."[14] He further holds that we all sin because we are all joint-inheritors of something called "original sin." This issue is first touched upon by Peck in *The Road Less Traveled* and, since the book remains on the market, we must assume that he still endorses what it has to say on the subject. Consequently, a brief look at Peck's first bestseller is necessary before examining *People of the Lie*.

Out of the Garden

According to *The Road Less Traveled*, "original sin" is nowhere more apparent than in the biblical story of Adam and Eve. This does not mean that Peck believes the account accurately relates an historical event. He sees it as merely a "myth" intended to convey some hidden truth.[15] Peck uses similar language in reference to the Mormon myth regarding the origins of man and the plan of salvation as contained in Mormonism's extrabiblical texts (i.e., the *Doctrine and Covenants* and *The Pearl of Great Price*).[16]

Peck believes that the key to understanding the Judeo-Christian myth of Adam and Eve lies in "what is missing" from the story.[17] It is significant to Peck that neither Adam nor Eve ever approach God to discuss the comments made by the serpent about the tree of knowledge: "They listened to the serpent, but they failed to get God's side of the story before they acted."[18]

According to Peck, the entire account symbolically points to a missing "step of debate" between God and the serpent.[19] This encounter is allegedly the "essence" of all sin.[20]

> The [missing] debate between the serpent and God is symbolic of the dialogue between good and evil which can and should occur within the minds of human beings. Our failure to conduct—or to conduct fully and wholeheartedly—this internal debate between good and evil is the cause of those evil actions that constitute sin.[21]

Some readers may fail to see how Peck can equate—even symbolically—a debate between God and the serpent with a debate within our own minds. It must be remembered that to Peck, God is not a personal entity separate from man. God is the collective unconscious permeating every person. The debate missing from the Genesis account symbolizes an internal debate because we are not only the source of evil intent, but we are also God.

> Human beings routinely fail to obtain God's side of the issue. They fail to consult or listen to the God within them, the knowledge of rightness which inherently resides within the minds of all mankind.[22]

Peck additionally states that we fail to hold internal debates with ourselves (the "God" within) because like "Adam and Eve, and every one of our ancestors before us, we are all lazy."[23] This laziness, says Peck, is original sin, and all of us have it.

> In the struggle to help my patients grow, I found that my chief enemy was invariably their laziness. And I became aware in myself of a similar reluctance to extend myself. . . . One thing I clearly had in common with all mankind was my laziness. It was at this point that the serpent-and-the-apple story suddenly made sense. . . . So original sin does exist; it is our laziness. . . . It exists in each and every one of us.[24]

Although Peck speaks a great deal about sin in *The Road Less Traveled*, he refrains from making in-depth remarks concerning evil. In *People of the Lie*, however, he fully articulates his views on evil and how it is connected to sin. Consequently, we now turn our attention to his second bestseller.

A Psychology of Evil

"The problem of evil is a very big mystery indeed," writes Peck in *People of the Lie*.[25] He further observes that because the very word " 'evil' requires an a priori [assumption-based] value judgment," it is a mystery which value-free science has chosen to ignore.[26] For a number of reasons, says Peck, this separation of religion and science simply does not work and the time has come for their reintegration.[27]

Part of the reintegration process must include what Peck calls a "psychology of evil" because evil is a reality that cannot be ignored. Unfortunately, "we do not yet have a body of scientific knowledge about human evil deserving of being called a psychology."[28] Peck attempts to remedy this, at least to some extent, through *People of the Lie*. His goal for wanting to form a psychology of evil is admirable.

> The only valid reason to recognize human evil is to heal it wherever we can, and . . . when we cannot, to study it further that we might discover how to heal it in specific instances and eventually wipe its ugliness off the face of the earth.[29]

According to Peck, a scientific psychology of evil must be three things. First, it must be a "healing" psychology. This is very important to Peck, as the above quote demonstrates.

Second, it must be an "integrated" psychology in that it is not restricted to information gleaned through purely scientific means. The new psychology of evil must be open to information from other sources, especially "mythology." Peck feels that as human beings have battled evil throughout the ages, they have "consciously or unconsciously incorporated the lessons they learned into mythic stories."[30]

Third, a psychology of evil must be religious. Peck does

not mean that this new psychology should embrace a "specific theology." Instead, it should "embrace valid insights from all religious traditions" and "recognize the reality of the 'supernatural.' "[31]

Peck proceeds to build his "new psychology" from scratch, noting that it is "a reflection of the enormous mystery of the subject that we do not have a generally accepted definition of evil."[32] The definition Peck ends up using was inspired by a few words his eight-year-old son uttered. "Why, Daddy," said the boy, "evil is 'live' spelled backward."[33] Peck could only agree.

> I can do no better than to heed my son. . . . Evil
> is in opposition to life. It is that which opposes
> the life force. It has, in short, to do with killing.
> Specifically, it has to do with murder. . . . I do
> not mean to restrict myself to corporeal murder.
> Evil is also that which kills spirit.[34]

To Peck, there are several essential attributes to life—"sentience, mobility, awareness, growth, autonomy, will."[35] If the body or any of these qualities are killed, then an "evil" act has taken place. In short, evil "is that force, residing either inside or outside of human beings, that seeks to kill life or liveliness."[36] Evil is related to sin because "evil is laziness [original sin] carried to its ultimate, extraordinary extreme."[37]

But evil needs an instrument through which to work. Such instruments are "evil" people. Peck is careful to note that one must use caution in labeling someone as evil. To distinguish between evil people and nonevil people, one must take into consideration their actions. Here Peck points out a difference between truly evil persons and those who just commit "ordinary sin."[38]

Sins per se do not characterize someone as evil, he says, "rather it is the subtlety and persistence and consistency of their sins. This is because the central defect of the evil [person] is not the sin but the refusal to acknowledge it."[39] Peck goes so far as to say that evil people "cannot be defined by the illegality of their deeds or the magnitude of their sins," but should be defined "by the consistency of their sins."[40]

Yet even hardened criminals who consistently sin are not evil. As Peck puts it, "there is a kind of randomness to their destructiveness" and "there is still a quality of openness to their wickedness."[41] On the other hand, truly evil people do not only sin consistently, but are covert and calculating about their sinful acts. A number of other characteristics are also present in evil persons.

1. An absolute "refusal to tolerate the sense of their own sinfulness," which causes them to become "uncorrectable grab bags of sin."[42]
2. A destructive nature that focuses on destroying others rather than "destroying the sickness within themselves."[43]
3. A self-image of perfection that will be preserved at all costs.[44]
4. An aversion to psychotherapy because evil people "hate the light—the light of goodness that shows them up, the light of scrutiny that exposes them, the light of truth that penetrates their deception. Psychotherapy is a light-shedding process par excellence."[45]

According to Peck, genuinely evil people are also "chronic scapegoaters." In other words, they are always blaming and attacking others "instead of facing their own failures."[46]

Moreover, they are secretive and underhanded about their deeds and tend to hide their sins under a facade of moral purity.[47] They are experts at disguising themselves,[48] and it is through the lies they propagate about themselves and others that they confuse the unwary. Hence, the title of Peck's second book.

> There is another reaction that the evil fre-
> quently engender in us: confusion. . . . Once
> again, this reaction is quite appropriate. Lies
> confuse. The evil are "the people of the lie," de-
> ceiving others as they also build layer upon
> layer of self-deception.[49]

After making these observations, Peck refers back to a
section of *The Road Less Traveled* where he defines evil as
"the imposition of one's will upon others by overt or covert
coercion—in order to avoid extending one's self for the
purpose of spiritual growth."[50]

What is actually being said here is that evil people are
those who refuse to progress toward "spiritual growth,"
which the reader will recall is defined by Peck as movement toward the realization that we are all God: "I have
said that the ultimate goal of spiritual growth is for the individual to become as one with God."[51]

Peck's most controversial beliefs about evil revolve
around his notion that evil people are really just mentally
ill because evil itself—or the force that seeks to kill—is
nothing more than a "mental illness."[52] It is simply a "psychological problem"; specifically, a variety of narcissism, or
"self-absorption," which is commonly referred to as "self-
love."[53]

It's All in Your Head

Because evil is a mental illness, it only stands to reason
that evil people are not born evil but become that way over
time. Peck gleans this from *The Heart of Man: Its Genius for
Good and Evil* by sociologist and psychologist Erich
Fromm (1900–1980).

> Fromm saw the genesis of human evil as a de-
> velopmental process: we are not created evil or
> forced to be evil, but we become evil slowly over

45

time through a long series of choices. I applaud his view.[54]

In summary, Peck notes, "to a greater or lesser degree, all mentally healthy individuals submit themselves to the demands of their own conscience."[55] Not so with the evil, however: "Evil is a very mysterious subject. People who are evil, as far as I can discern, have a conscience but refuse to use it."[56]

This clearly reflects what Peck said in *The Road Less Traveled*: "[M]ental illness occurs when the conscious will of the individual deviates substantially from the will of God, which is the individual's own unconscious will."[57]

What causes the mental illness of evil? According to Peck, an individual's evil "can almost always be traced to some extent to his or her childhood circumstances, the sins of the parents and the nature of their heredity."[58] Hope for evil people resides in the same place as does hope for the physically diseased—with healing professionals.

> I do not think we shall come any closer than we are today to understanding and, I hope, curing human evil until the healing professions name evil as an illness within the domain of their professional responsibilities.[59]

By labeling evil as a mental illness, Peck again identifies as evil those people who will not listen to their "God" within, or who do not recognize their own inner divinity. Mental health, or goodness, is manifested by listening to our internal godness. This is clear in a reference that Peck makes to a recovering psychiatric patient: "But Billie is doing it," writes Peck. "In the name of God *or her true self* she is somehow beginning to separate from her mother. . . . [emphasis added]"[60] The lines Peck draws are crystal clear.

There are only two states of being: submission to God [the collective unconscious] and goodness or the refusal to submit to anything beyond one's own will—which refusal automatically enslaves one to the forces of evil. We must ultimately belong either to God [the collective unconscious] or the devil.[61]

Noteworthy here is the acknowledgment of the devil. That Peck would mention Satan at some point in *People of the Lie* is only natural. He rightly observes, "the issue of evil inevitably raises the question of the devil."[62] In the following section, we will explore Peck's views concerning that ancient entity known as Satan.

The Devil Made Me Do It

Who exactly is Satan? In the latter half of *People of the Lie*, Peck responds to this question with blunt honesty: "I don't know."[63] What he does know, however, is that Satan is an actual "being" of immaterial spirit that possesses an unbelievably evil personality pervaded by "an active presence of hate."[64]

He knows all of this from personal experience—specifically, face-to-face encounters with the devil during two exorcisms he allegedly attended: "The vast majority of [demonic possession] cases described in the literature are those of possession by minor demons. These two were highly unusual in that both were cases of Satanic possession. I now know Satan is real."[65]

Peck originally did not believe in either demonic possession or the devil, but as an "open-minded scientist" he remained willing to look at any evidence that might challenge his view. In 15 years of psychiatric practice, however, he had never once "seen anything faintly resembling a case."[66]

He decided to search for a case and found three. Two of them were nothing but examples of people suffering from "standard psychiatric disorders." The third one, however, "turned out to be the real thing."[67] He eventually stumbled across a second bona fide case of possession. According to Peck, both individuals were possessed by "a spirit that has been well described in Christian literature under the name of Satan."[68]

The stories recounted by Peck rival the best of modern-day horror movies. During one exorcism the devil reportedly spoke as "an expression appeared on the patient's face that could be described only as Satanic. It was an incredibly contemptuous grin of utter hostile malevolence."[69]

When Satan was revealed in the other patient, Peck claims that a hissing voice was accompanied by an even more ghastly expression.

> The patient suddenly resembled a writhing snake of great strength, viciously attempting to bite the team members. More frightening than the writhing body, however, was the face. The eyes were hooded with lazy reptilian torpor—except when the reptile darted out in attack, at which moment the eyes would open wide with blazing hatred.[70]

Peck testifies that almost all of the team members at both exorcisms "were convinced they were at these times in the presence of something absolutely alien and inhuman."[71] Only when the evil presence departed from the patient and the room did the exorcisms end.

Whether or not these exorcisms ever really occurred is difficult to know. Peck does not give the names of the afflicted persons. Nor does he say where the exorcisms were held. He does not even identify individuals able to corroborate his stories. In any case, Peck points to these experiences as the source of substantial bits of information about the devil.

Peck also acknowledges that much of his knowledge about Satan is based on what he calls "Judeo-Christian myth and doctrine about Satan."[72] According to his understanding of this myth, Satan was originally "God's second-in-command, chief among all His angels, the beautiful and beloved Lucifer."[73]

The original "service" Satan performed "in God's behalf" was supposedly the testing and temptation of human beings. This was done in order to enhance spiritual growth—"just as we test our own children in school so as to enhance their growth."[74] The devil was "primarily a teacher of mankind," as evidenced by the name Lucifer, which means "the light bearer."[75]

All was fine until the devil started tempting and testing humanity out of sheer delight, rather than on God's behalf. "This we see," writes Peck, "in the Book of Job."[76] What allegedly happened next directly caused the current state of war between God and the devil.

> . . . God decided that something more was required than simple testing for the uplifting of mankind; what was required was both an example of His love and an example to live by. So He sent His only son to live and die as one of us. Satan was superseded by Christ both in function and in God's heart.[77]

"Satan perceived this as an intolerable personal insult," so the story goes. Eventually, the devil became puffed up with pride, rebelled against God, and made heaven a place "not big enough for the both of them."[78] Satan was subsequently cast into hell. There, the avowed enemy of God "dreams of revenge" and wages a "war against God's design" through seeking to destroy mankind.[79]

To add some plausibility to this tale, Peck appeals to the original meanings behind the words "satan" and "devil."

> The original meaning of the words "satan" and "devil" were not pejorative, as they are today.

> "Devil" and "diabolic" come from the Greek
> verb *diabalein*, meaning simply "to oppose." The
> word "satan" commonly meant "adversary." In
> the Book of Numbers, God Himself stated that
> He was proceeding against Balaam as a satan.
> Seeing the necessity for mankind to be tested
> and tempted by something in *opposition* to His
> own will, God delegated this oppositional (dia-
> bolic) and adversarial (satanic) function to the
> chief of His archangels.[80]

The language here is confusing at best because Peck consistently refers to God in a manner that suggests that the
supreme deity is a personal entity outside of and totally
separate from man. Peck never explains how this can be,
given his belief that God is the "collective unconscious" of
man. Nor does he state which parts of the above story he
believes to be true, or how he arrived at his interpretation
of the biblical texts.

A possible explanation may lie in another notion Peck has
about the devil—Satan is an "it." This may again seem contradictory to other comments made by Peck, but his reasons
for describing the devil as an "it" make sense if taken in light
of his view of "God." It all has to do with sexuality.

> I shall . . . use the neuter for Satan. While I
> know Satan to be lustful to penetrate us, I have
> not in the least experienced this desire as sexual
> or creative—only hateful and destructive.[81]

In contrast to Satan, God "is not neuter," says Peck. "He
is exploding with life and love—even sexuality of a sort. So
'It' is not appropriate."[82] Peck prefers to use the pronoun
"He" for God because God "desires to penetrate us" and
"chases after us with a vigor in the hunt that we most typically associate with males."[83]

All of this may cast some light on how Peck can refer to

God in personal terms even though God is supposedly nothing more than man's collective unconscious mind. Since we are sexual beings, then our unconscious is also sexual, which in turn means God is sexual, and in that way, personal. In other words, our unconscious is always "after us" as a man might pursue a woman.

Peck never explains his views in such an orderly manner. Of course, it may be that he has another explanation for referring to God in personal terms while at the same time viewing God as our collective unconscious. If so, that explanation is never given. There is also always the possibility that his comments about God are simply an inconsistency on his part.

In either case, one thing is clear to Peck. Although Satan is a truly personal entity, Satan does not display sexuality. Consequently, the devil is more properly termed an "it." Peck regularly refers to Satan in this way, blending personal attributes with the use of the impersonal "it":

> Satan does not easily let go. After *its* expulsion *it* seems to hang around. . . . Satan will not only tell the patient *it* is still around but in one case repeatedly misled the patient into believing that *it* was still inside. . . . Satan can manifest *itself* in and through material beings, but *it itself* is not material. . . . *It* is spirit [emphasis added].[84]

Peck claims that through the exorcisms that he witnessed he found out that the devil is literally the antichrist.

> Where once it [Satan] existed to spiritually uplift mankind, it now exists to spiritually destroy us. . . . Satan perceives Christ as its personal enemy. . . . Satan [is] the living Antichrist. . . . When asked in one exorcism why it was the Antichrist, it answered, "Because Christ taught people to love each other."[85]

51

But as evil as the devil is, says Peck, "it" cannot do evil except "through a human body. . . . It does not have the power to kill or even harm by itself. It must use human beings to do its deviltry."[86] In other words, if a terrible deed is going to be done by Satan, "human hands" must be used.[87] Peck also maintains that because Satan has no real power without a human body, all of his threats are hollow lies. In fact, *the only power that Satan has is through human belief in its lies.*[88] Hence, Peck's favorite epithet for the devil—the Father of Lies.[89]

In addition to being the Father of Lies, Satan "may be said to be a spirit of mental illness."[90] Peck feels this way because mental health, as defined in *The Road Less Traveled* and *People of the Lie*, is "an ongoing process of dedication to reality at all costs."[91] Satan is utterly opposed to that process, which gives Peck the best definition he claims to have for the devil—*a real spirit of unreality.*[92]

Peck goes on to argue that because Satan uses lies so effectively, possessed individuals are not necessarily evil in and of themselves. Peck even "admired" both of the possessed persons he met and suspects that "the potential holiness of these two people was one of the reasons for their possession."[93]

Personal character and a willingness to be freed are crucial to a successful exorcism, writes Peck. Ultimately, he says, "it is the patient herself or himself who is the exorcist."[94] After all, God "cannot heal a person who does not want to be healed."[95] He explains:

> At the moment of expulsion [of Satan] both these patients voluntarily took the crucifix, held it to their chests and prayed for deliverance. Both chose that moment to cast their lots with God.[96]

This does not mean that others are not needed in order for someone to be rid of a demon or Satan. On the contrary, sometimes an entire team is required, a team that may, or may not, consist of Christians. What a person believes theologically appears to be relatively unimportant to Peck.[97]

The Exorcists

In saying that the patient is ultimately the exorcist, Peck is careful to assure readers that he is not denigrating the role of the exorcist proper, which is "a heroic one." An exorcist's character must be marked by gentleness, caring, patience, discernment and a willingness to suffer. These qualities enable him or her to lead the exorcism from beginning to end.[98] Assistants to the exorcist are often present as well. In fact, Peck has found that exorcisms are "always conducted by a team of at least three or more. In a sense the team 'gangs up' on the patient."[99]

Because there is so much raw power present during an exorcism, Peck considers the procedure a dangerous one that should only be attempted by carefully selected individuals. The key to choosing good team members is their level of love, which is defined by Peck as the will to "extend one's self for the purpose of nurturing one's own or another's spiritual growth."[100]

The "greatest safeguard is love," writes Peck.[101] Indeed, "in all serious cases more is required than knowledge and skill; it is only love that can heal."[102] This prerequisite of love is non-negotiable because "the presence of one unloving person in the room is likely not only to cause the exorcism to fail but to subject the team members as well as the patient to the possibility of grave harm."[103]

Peck is certainly no respecter of persons when it comes to who is and who is not loving. Everyone is potentially a legitimate candidate for an exorcism team.

> Were I to conduct an exorcism, I would not exclude from the team any mature Hindu, Buddhist, Muslim, Jew, atheist, or agnostic who was a genuinely loving presence. But I would with-

out hesitation exclude a nominal Christian or anyone else who was not such a [loving] presence.[104]

God's presence at an exorcism is very important, says Peck. This is why anyone, regardless of their theological beliefs, can be a part of the procedure: "I suspect that whenever seven to ten people gather together at personal risk, motivated by love and healing, God will be there . . . and that healing will occur."[105]

A loving team is also extremely important because during an exorcism the patient is given their very first experience of "community," which basically occurs when persons are gathered together in mutual total acceptance, openness, honesty and love.[106] (The subject of community is further explained in chapter 5.) A footnote Peck writes to this last point includes an especially significant piece of information.

[D]espite the fact that some team members were self-defined atheists or admittedly lukewarm Christians, there is no doubt in my mind that at each exorcism the team assembled was a true "Christian community."[107]

Peck not only reveals that atheists were on his exorcism teams, but that these unbelievers and "lukewarm" Christians were able to still make a "Christian" community. Peck is hinting at something here that we have not yet explored—his definition of a Christian.

The following chapter will demonstrate that Peck's definition of a Christian differs radically from conventional ideas. To Peck, being a Christian has little to do with what one believes doctrinally. Although a self-professed Christian, Peck himself holds a number of beliefs not normally found within the Christian church. As we shall now see, some of these beliefs are quite shocking.

Endnotes

1. Peck, M. Scott. *People of the Lie* (New York: Simon & Schuster, 1983), back cover endorsement.

2. Peck, p. 11.

3. Patterson, Ben. "Is God a Psychotherapist?," *Christianity Today*, March 1, 1985, p. 23.

4. Howard, Walden. "One Thing is Simple in Scott Peck's Difficult World," *News from Faith at Work*, July 1981, p. 5.

5. Howard, p. 5.

6. Bolotin, Susan. "God & Freud," *Vogue*, December 1985, p. 317; cf. "Spiritual-Growth Evangelism: Path to World Peace?" by John Dart, *Los Angeles Times*, June 17, 1987, p. 1.

7. Patterson, p. 21.

8. Dart, p. 4.

9. Howard, p. 5.

10. Howard, p. 5; cf. Dart, p. 4.

11: Connors, Diane. "M. Scott Peck," *Omni*, October 1988, p. 126.

12. Patterson, p. 21.

13. Peck, p. 70.

14. Peck, p. 71.

15. Peck, M. Scott. *The Road Less Traveled* (New York: Simon & Schuster, 1978), p. 274.

16. Peck, *People*, p. 78.

17. Peck, *The Road*, p. 272.

18. Peck, *The Road*, p. 272.

19. Peck, *The Road*, p. 272.

20. Peck, *The Road*, p. 272.

21. Peck, *The Road*, p. 273.

22. Peck, *The Road*, p. 273.

23. Peck, *The Road*, p. 273.

24. Peck, *The Road*, pp. 272, 273.

25. Peck, *People*, p. 41.

26. Peck, *People*, p. 40.

27. Peck, *People*, p. 40.

28. Peck, *People*, p. 39.

29. Peck, *People*, p. 44.

30. Peck, *People*, pp. 44–45.

31. Peck, *People*, p. 45.

32. Peck, *People*, p. 42.

33. Peck, *People*, p. 42.

34. Peck, *People*, p. 42.

35. Peck, *People*, p. 42.

36. Peck, *People*, p. 43.

37. Peck, *The Road*, p. 278.

38. Peck, *People*, p. 69.

39. Peck, *People*, p. 69.

40. Peck, *People*, p. 71.

41. Peck, *People*, pp. 69, 70.

42. Peck, *People*, pp. 71, 72.

43. Peck, *People*, p. 74.

44. Peck, *People*, p. 74.

45. Peck, *People*, p. 77.

46. Peck, *People*, p. 74.

47. Peck, *People*, p. 69, 75.

48. Peck, *People*, p. 76.

49. Peck, *People*, p. 66.

50. Peck, *People*, p. 74; cf. *The Road Less Traveled* by M. Scott Peck, p. 278.

51. Peck, *The Road*, pp. 282–283.

52. Peck, *People*, p. 121.

53. Peck, *People*, p. 77.

54. Peck, *People*, p. 82.

55. Peck, *People*, p. 78.

56. Scheinin, Richard. "Author M. Scott Peck Challenges Our Notions of Love and Spiritual Growth," *San Jose Mercury News*, February 19, 1991, p. 8D.

57. Peck, *The Road*, p. 282.

58. Peck, *People*, p. 126.

59. Peck, *People*, p. 127.

60. Peck, *People*, p. 148.

61. Peck, *People*, p. 83.

62. Peck, *People*, p. 42.

63. Peck, *People*, p. 203.

64. Peck, *People*, pp. 206, 207, 208.

65. Peck, *People*, p. 183.

66. Peck, *People*, p. 182.

67. Peck, *People*, p. 183.

68. Peck, *People*, p. 201.

69. Peck, *People*, p. 196.

70. Peck, *People*, p. 196.

71. Peck, *People*, p. 196.

72. Peck, *People*, p. 203.

73. Peck, *People*, p. 203.

74. Peck, *People*, p. 203.

75. Peck, *People*, p. 203.

76. Peck, *People*, p. 203.

77. Peck, *People*, p. 203.

78. Peck, *People*, p. 203.

79. Peck, *People*, pp. 203–204.

80. Peck, *People*, p. 203.

81. Peck, *People*, p. 12.

82. Peck, *People*, p. 12.

83. Peck, *People*, p. 12.

84. Peck, *People*, pp. 197, 198, 206.

85. Peck, *People*, p. 204.

86. Peck, *People*, p. 206.

87. Peck, *People*, p. 206.

88. Peck, *People*, p. 206.

89. Peck, *People*, p. 207.

90. Peck, *People*, p. 207.

91. Peck, *People*, p. 207.

92. Peck, *People*, p. 207.

93. Peck, *People*, p. 194.

94. Peck, *People*, p. 197.

95. Peck, *People*, p. 197.

96. Peck, *People*, p. 197.

97. Peck, *People*, p. 189.

98. Peck, *People*, p. 197.

99. Peck, *People*, p. 186.

100. Peck, *The Road*, p. 81.

101. Peck, *People*, p. 188.

102. Peck, *People*, p. 188.

103. Peck, *People*, p. 201.

104. Peck, *People*, p. 201.

105. Peck, *People*, p. 199.

106. Peck, *The Different Drum* (New York: Simon & Schuster, 1987), pp. 86–165.

107. Peck, *People*, p. 199.

CHAPTER 3

In the Name of God

*In main stream churches and New Age seminars, at
12-step meetings and along the recovery aisles of
bookstores, Peck is a figure of comfort and affirma-
tion.*

—Life Magazine[1]

Many Christians and non-Christians alike have accepted Peck's conversion to Christianity as genuine. He is regularly billed as a Christian writer, Christian
psychiatrist and Christian leader.[2] He has even been
grouped with such well-known evangelicals as Chuck
Swindoll and James Dobson.[3] Is it legitimate to catego-
rize Peck in this way? Are his religious beliefs consistent
with Christianity? Do his teachings reflect the teachings
of Jesus Christ?

This chapter will focus on Peck's doctrinal positions. I
will draw from his many books, as well as from several interviews he has given. As we shall see, Peck promotes a
number of beliefs inconsistent with Christianity. He himself confesses, "[T]here are many ways that I deviate from
traditional Christianity."[4]

God's Book of Myths

Christians worldwide name the Bible as their source of truth. M. Scott Peck does so as well, often quoting Scripture and using it to substantiate his beliefs. As noted in chapter 2, Peck believes the story of Adam and Eve is a "myth." Unfortunately, the Garden of Eden saga is not the only portion of Scripture that Peck relegates to a less than historically accurate position.

> [The Bible] is a mixture of legend, some of which is true and some of which is not true. It is a mixture of very accurate history and not so accurate history. It is a mixture of outdated rules and some pretty good rules. It is a mixture of myth and metaphor.[5]

Peck acknowledges that many Christians disagree with him, believing instead that the Bible is God's inerrant and infallible Word. Peck labels such persons "fundamentalists." At the same time, he maintains that the term is really a misnomer, and that a more accurate word is " 'inerrantists,' those who believe that the Bible is not only the divinely inspired word of God but the actual transcribed, unaltered word of God."[6] To Peck's mind, such thinking "only impoverishes the Bible."[7] He further observes that these inerrantists "strangely misuse the Bible."[8]

Peck's views may be linked to his understanding that everyone who believes the Bible is God's Word also believes that all Scripture must be interpreted in a rigidly literal way. Inerrantists, he says, completely dismiss the possibility that some verses should be taken allegorically or metaphorically.[9]

As an example of how all inerrantists interpret Scripture, Peck cites the case of a young man who gouged out one of his eyes in obedience to Jesus' words: "if your eye causes you to sin, pluck it out" (Mark 9:47).[10] Peck further intimates that all inerrantists are somewhat haughty and arrogant.

> The inerrantist . . . is somebody who believes the Bible is not only the divinely inspired word of God, but the *literal* word of God and that it should be interpreted literally and that there is really only one proper interpretation—namely theirs.[11]

Rather than submit to such a backward method of biblical interpretation, Peck chooses to read Scripture as mythology. Myths supposedly "speak more eloquently to the truth of the human condition than do other kinds of prose."[12] In fact, "a myth is myth precisely because it is true. . . . And because they have much to teach us about human nature, myths can be extremely useful for understanding ourselves."[13]

Peck cites dragons as one example of a myth. For centuries these mythological creatures have provided inspiration for countless fairy tales, bedtime stories and novels. As far back as medieval times, Christian monks were "illuminating dragons on the margins of the manuscripts they were painstakingly copying."[14]

Dragons are also recognized worldwide. History is replete with dragon-adorned documents made by Chinese Taoists monks, Japanese Buddhists, Hindus from India and Muslims from Arabia. Why? Peck proposes that they are "human-being symbols."[15] He explains further:

> They [dragons] are snakes with wings. Worms that can fly. And that's us. So, reptilelike, we slink close to the ground, mired in the mud of our sinful proclivities and narrow-minded cultural prejudices. And yet like birds—or angels—we have the capacity to soar in the

heavens and transcend those same sinful pro-
clivities and narrow-minded cultural prejudices.[16]

Taking the mythological view of Scripture allows Peck
to reject the meaning of the biblical words themselves in
favor of any one of a countless number of alternate inter-
pretations. The mythological method of Bible reading also
enables Peck to find "hidden" messages that may have
nothing to do with either the context, grammar or cultural
setting of a passage.

To this mythical view of the Bible, Peck adds the notion that Scripture is full of innumerable errors and outdated rules. What remains is a book that can be made to
say virtually anything. This is perhaps most evident in
his perceptions of the pivotal character of Scripture—Jesus Christ.

Another Jesus

The Jesus that emerges from the writings of M. Scott
Peck bears little resemblance to the Jesus that has historically been worshiped by the Christian church. To Peck,
"Jesus was an example of the Western mystic."[17] It is difficult to know exactly what Peck means here because a
stereotypical "mystic" does not exist. Even a precise definition of "mysticism" is lacking.

In general, the term *mysticism* is meant to describe "an
experienced, direct, nonabstract, unmediated, loving knowing of God, a knowing or seeing so direct as to be called union with God."[18] Explanations of what it means to practice
mysticism vary. Some would apply all communion with
God as mystical while others would limit mystical encounters to those experiences marked by an especially profound
encounter with God.

Mysticism is usually marked by an acquisition of
knowledge not simply through divine revelation, but

through actual union with the divine. Because it transcends the cognitive part of man, this union imparts knowledge directly to the soul. In other words, it bypasses the mind. Consequently, rather than saying they "believe" something to be so, mystics will instead say they "know" something is so.

A sense of union or oneness with all reality is also commonly acknowledged by mystics. Losing the individual self to the greater or larger reality is the end goal. In fact, it is through such a union that truth is obtained. These characteristics of a mystic are evident in the Jesus described by Peck.

> He integrated himself with God: "I am in the Father and the Father in Me." He blurred the distinction between himself and others: "Inasmuch as you have done it unto one of the least of these . . . ye have done it unto me." . . . Finally, he gave . . . the proper paradoxical attitude toward the self when he proclaimed, "Whosoever will save his life [self] will lose it, and whosoever will lose his life [self] for my sake [i.e., in the right way] will find it."[19]

Jesus allegedly had a mindset in common not only with Jewish mystics before Him, but also with Christian, Jewish and Muslim mystics after Him.[20] This view is consistent with Peck's habit of regularly placing Jesus on a level no higher than all other historical religious figures.

In his 1993 book *A World Waiting to Be Born*, Peck categorizes Jesus as simply a great prophet on par with Moses, Isaiah, Mohammed "and other prophets and martyrs since."[21] During a 1992 interview, Peck commented that religions are usually started by "very holy people—say, Buddha and Jesus and Lao-tzu [founder of Taoism]."[22]

In *Further Along the Road Less Traveled*, Peck places the founders of the world's major religions on equal footing because they all taught the notion of loving one's neighbor. Included in the list of comparable figures are "Jesus, Buddha, Krishna, Confucius, and Muhammad."[23]

Peck also promotes a rather unconventional view of Jesus' character, personality and temperament. He often accuses the Christian church—specifically "three-fourths" of all Christians—of presenting what his wife Lily has dubbed "the wimpy Jesus."[24] This false representation of Christ is nothing but a " 'mellow-yellow, peace and love' consciousness"[25] who went around "with this sweet smile on his face, doing very little other than patting children on the head."[26]

"But that's not at all the Jesus of the Gospels," Peck assures everyone.[27] The *real* Jesus was supposedly very much like any other person. He "wasn't terribly happy."[28] Nor did He ever have "much peace of mind."[29] Jesus was also a "terribly, terribly lonely"[30] Man "who was often angry, scared, sad, or even prejudiced on occasion."[31] According to Peck the historical Jesus was "a man who was almost continually frustrated . . . sometimes depressed, frequently anxious and scared."[32]

Peck often tells a personal story that perfectly illustrates the kind of Jesus he follows. The episode happened before Peck obtained an unlisted telephone number.

> One night the phone rang. . . . [A]n elderly woman asked, "Are you the Dr. Peck who's going to be talking about sexuality and spirituality at St. Michael's Church Friday night?" "Yes, I am." "Good. I'm taking my husband. . . . [H]e says he's too old to have sex. I want you to tell him he should have sex with me." "That's not necessarily the subject of the talk," I said, "but if at the question-and-answer period you come up, I'd be happy to talk about it. I'm glad you're going and hope you enjoy it."[33]

After hanging up, Peck was left "with a bad feeling," irritated with both the woman and himself, but unsure of how he might have better handled the situation.[34] He then asked a thoughtful question: "Jesus, how would you have answered that phone call?"[35] Peck received an interesting revelation.

> The answer came to me with certainty. What Jesus would have said in essence was, "Lady, where the hell do you think you come off, calling me at home on a Wednesday night, trying to tell me what to lecture about on Friday night? It's the most arrogant, self-centered thing I've ever heard of. Maybe if you were a little less self-centered your husband might be a little more interested in you. Good night!" And then Jesus would have hung up the receiver with a certain definiteness to emphasize his point.[36]

Besides portraying Jesus as a rude individual, Peck adamantly states that Jesus was not interested in "family." In fact, Jesus was quite antifamily.

> This supposedly Christian culture emphasizes family values—the family that prays together stays together—as if Jesus had been some kind of a great family man. . . . [T]he fact is that the Jesus of the Gospels was not a great family man. If anything, he was a breaker-up of families. He set siblings against siblings and children against parents . . . because he was fighting against the idolatry of family—where family togetherness becomes sacred at all costs, where it becomes more important to do what will keep the family matriarch or patriarch happy than to do what God wants you to do."[37]

Peck's insight into Jesus' character is supposedly gleaned from the Gospels. This does not mean, however, that Peck believes the Gospels are in any way more accurate than the Old Testament. He goes out of his way to say that he does not "want to imply that the Gospels are totally accurate."[38] "Some things," asserts Peck, "obviously seem to have been added. Others seem to me to be obviously missing."[39]

What "things" is Peck talking about? First, Jesus' sense of humor is strangely absent. Second, Jesus' sexuality is missing as well. Peck says little about Jesus' humor, but makes some interesting observations about Jesus' sexuality.

He strongly intimates that Jesus was not only romantically interested in Mary Magdalene, but also may have had homosexual feelings for the Apostle John. Scripture's silence regarding Jesus' sexuality indicates to Peck that the world's Savior may have been bisexual, or to use Peck's word, "whole."

> . . . Jesus' sexuality seems to me rather ambiguous. He appears to have been very fond of Mary Magdalene, who might have been a prostitute, and He is frequently pictured in an intimate pose with the Apostle John, who is referred to as "the one whom Jesus loved." I believe that Jesus was an androgynous figure; that is, not without sex, or unisexed, but whole.[40]

Peck's Jesus was incredibly human. So human, in fact, that He did not even know He was the Messiah and, at some point, had to figure it out. Peck believes that the most likely time and place for Jesus' realization of His calling was the desert temptation.

> To me it is clear that Jesus went into the desert to wrestle with the problem of authority.

In being baptized by John, he is essentially told by both John and God that he is the Messiah. "Me, the Messiah?" he must have asked himself. "Where do I come off being the Messiah? I'd better go off alone and think this one over." So into the wilderness he went to face the issues.[41]

Even at the end of His ministry, Jesus was still terrorized by uncertainty and ignorance of His mission. In the Garden of Gethsemane, Jesus' choice to go to the cross was nothing more than a "murky judgment call" made in response to what just "felt right" inside. Peck bases this particular belief about Jesus on a bit of advice he received many years ago from a spiritual mentor.

Eight years ago . . . I made my only emergency phone call to my spiritual director. "God never calls someone to do something that doesn't feel *right* in his heart," she said. It was a piece of advice I have used a number of times since. . . . It is valid for many occasions. . . . When Jesus, for instance, sweating blood in sheer terror in the Garden of Gethsemane, accepted his calling to go to the cross . . . he did, I believe, choose the cross because it was the only alternative that felt right in his heart. . . . From time to time—not too often, mind you—we may be called to make some "radical response" to life. . . . [T]he call, as it did for Jesus, may feel quite murky. . . . [T]hese murky "judgment calls" . . . may have to be made repeatedly.[42]

One might well ask, "If Jesus was so unsure of himself, then why did he have to go to the cross at all?" According to Peck, Jesus' death was not necessarily to atone for sins. In fact, this view is Peck's "least popular" way of understanding why Jesus died.[43] Peck prefers to see Jesus as a perfect example of how to live and die.[44]

He points out that others besides Jesus have walked a similar road of suffering. In his search for truth, Buddha supposedly went through exactly what Jesus endured. "Buddha and Christ were not different men. The suffering of Christ letting go on the cross and the joy of Buddha letting go under the bo tree are one."[45] (The bo tree refers to the Bodhi tree, "the tree in India under which the historical Buddha, Siddhartha Gautama, sat until he attained enlightenment."[46])

Like other great religious leaders in history, Jesus and Buddha are examples for us to follow. Peck feels we can all suffer the way they did and, like them, find truth by letting go of ourselves. "We must not only realize that he [Jesus] in fact suffered all that we suffer, we must also realize that we in fact *can* suffer all that he suffered."[47] The whole sacrifice of Jesus was simply an example of one man's ability to throw Himself "into the Cloud of Unknowing and cast his being into the arms of the even to him unknowable God."[48]

Christians may find this information difficult to believe because Peck often refers to Jesus as both God and man. In *Further Along the Road Less Traveled*, he writes that Jesus was "paradoxically both human and divine . . . 'fully human and fully divine.' "[49] But what Peck actually means is something far different from what the words suggest.

According to Peck, Jesus was a human male who was simply indwelt by a larger proportion of God (the "collective unconscious"). This level of divinity is also attainable by us since we, too, have God indwelling our unconscious. "Jesus . . . like all of us (albeit in different proportions, apparently) had two parts to his mind: a divine part and a human part."[50]

Regarding Jesus' resurrection, Peck again takes a view uncommon to Christians. He sees the resurrection as merely a symbolic story signifying how Christ overcame evil.[51] Jesus was not really raised bodily from the grave. Christ is now a spirit. "As Christ in spirit lives, so is Satan the living Antichrist."[52]

Since Peck denies Jesus' bodily resurrection, it only makes sense that he would reject the physical Second Coming.

> When I think of the enormity of the changes required to bring about the end of the arms race . . . it sometimes seems that a virtual Second Coming is required. I am not talking about a bodily second coming. In fact, I am profoundly pessimistic about a Church that would sit around passively waiting for its messiah to appear again in the flesh. Rather, I am talking about the resurrection of Christ's spirit, which would occur in the Church if Christians took him seriously.[53]

Peck also dismisses the physical resurrection of all humanity. He states, "I find distasteful the traditional idea of Christianity which preaches the resurrection of the body. . . . I prefer to believe that souls can exist independently from bodies. I think it is possible for souls to exist independently of bodies and even to be developed independently of bodies."[54]

Although he denies the bodily resurrection, Peck accepts the idea that individuals continue to exist after death. His beliefs regarding what happens to the dead will now be examined.

The Other Side

When it comes to the subject of life after death, Peck remains uncommitted to a specific way of thinking. He seems to base his opinions on personal theories coupled with Protestant thought and Roman Catholic tradition. For example, he believes in the Roman Catholic and Greek Orthodox doctrine of purgatory. According to this belief, all Christians who die without having obtained a state of perfection (sinlessness) "go to purgatory [a spiritual realm of existence] where, for a longer or shorter time, they suffer until all sin is purged away, after which they are translated to heaven."[55]

Peck writes, "I imagine Purgatory as a very elegant, well-appointed psychiatric hospital with the most modern and highly developed techniques for making learning as gentle and painless as possible under divine supervision."[56]

When it comes to the nature of heaven, Peck admits that he knows little about it. He does believe, however, that heaven will be open to everyone regardless of their sex, race or religion. He knows this because God "loves variety," as evidenced by the many different kinds of people on earth.[57] Peck extrapolates from this that heaven will certainly "not conform to the stereotypical notion of identical cherubs with standard-issue halos and harps sitting around on fluffy clouds."[58]

The Christian concept of hell is utterly rejected by Peck. "I simply cannot accept the view of Hell in which God punishes people without hope and destroys souls without a chance for redemption."[59] He further asserts that God "wouldn't go to the trouble of creating souls, with all their complexity, just to fry them in the end."[60] (Again, the reader should remember that when Peck says "God," he means the collective unconscious mind of man, not "God" as in a personal entity separate from humanity.)

Peck has his own idea of hell. He maintains that it exists right here on earth. Evil people, he explains, are "[f]orever fleeing the light of self-exposure and the voice of their own conscience."[61] Consequently, they "live their lives in sheer terror." Such people "need not be consigned to any hell; they are already in it."[62] As Peck says, "God does not punish; we punish ourselves."[63]

Hope is available, however, for those persons living in their self-made hell. According to Peck, they "can walk right out of Hell."[64] Unfortunately, many do not do so.

> Those who are in hell are there by their own choice. Indeed, they could walk right out of it if they so chose, except that their values are such as to make the path out of hell appear overwhelmingly dangerous, frighteningly painful, and impossibly difficult. So they remain in hell because it seems safe and easy to them. . . . The notion that people are in hell by their own choice is not widely familiar, but the fact is that it is both good psychology and good theology."[65]

In reference to his concept of hell, Peck rightly comments, "I know that is not traditional Christianity."[66] A number of other doctrines held by Peck are also not "traditional Christianity." Let us consider his view of humanity.

Paradise Lost, Evolution Gained

"The story of the Garden of Eden is, of course, a myth," says Peck. "But like other myths, it is an embodiment of truth."[67] Peck further maintains that "although the fundamentalists—the inerrantists and creationists—may not like it, one of the things that the Eden myth teaches us about is evolution. . . . Genesis 3 is a myth about how we human beings evolved into consciousness."[68] He explains:

> When we ate the apple from the Tree of the Knowledge of Good and Evil, we became conscious, and having become conscious, we immediately became self-conscious. . . . When this

71

happened to us, we became conscious of ourselves as separate entities. We lost the sense of
oneness with nature, with the rest of the universe.[69]

Humanity's ego separation from the universe is supposedly the reason why so many people are shy, or "self-con-
scious." Peck holds that to be human is to be shy and vice
versa. Anyone who is not shy has a major problem.

So one of the things this myth tells us is that it
is human to be shy. . . . I have never met such a
person [a wonderful, deep-thinking person]
who was not basically shy. . . . [T]he very few
people I have met who were not shy were people
who had been damaged in some way, who had
lost some of their humanity.[70]

Herein lies the chief end of man according to Peck—
lose self-consciousness, merge with the unconscious and
regain our sense of oneness with the universe, our godhood. We must return to Eden so to speak. This is salvation.

[W]hile consciousness is the whole cause of
pain, it is also the cause of our salvation, because salvation is the process of becoming in-
creasingly conscious. . . . [T]he purpose of
psychotherapy—healing of the psyche—was to
make the unconscious conscious; that is, to in-
crease consciousness.[71] Since the unconscious
is God all along, we may further define the
goal of spiritual growth to be the attainment of
godhood by the conscious self. It is for the individual to become totally, wholly God. . . .
The point is to become God while preserving
consciousness. . . . [I]t is to develop a mature,

conscious ego which then can become the ego of God.[72]

Reaching spiritual growth through psychological growth is possible, says Peck, because there is no difference between the mind and the spirit. They are one and the same. He makes absolutely "no distinction between the mind and the spirit, and therefore no distinction between the process of achieving spiritual growth and achieving mental growth."[73]

To Peck, then, all psychological "healing" is the very process of salvation.

> [T]he word *salvation* means 'healing,' " he declares. "It comes from the same word as *salve*. . . . Salvation is the process of healing and the process of becoming whole. And health, wholeness, and holiness are all derived from the same root. They all mean virtually the same thing.[74]

In other words, salvation is obtained through psychological healing. Psychological healing—also known as spiritual growth—occurs as we get more in touch with our unconscious mind, which is God. As we make our unconscious mind more conscious, we eventually come to consciously realize that which our unconscious mind already knows—we are God.

Peck's concept of God has already been discussed, but a further examination must be made of the way he consistently, or rather inconsistently, refers to God. His comments have confused a number of individuals, especially Christians.

God: He, She or It?

We have seen that Peck believes God to be the "collective unconscious" mind of humanity. This is confirmed in his 1993 book *A World Waiting to Be Born,* which asserts that we can "choose to hear and attend to the still small voice of conscience or God."[75]

Recently, Peck has embraced process theology, which teaches among other things, that God—however defined—is in the process of change, as is all life. This fits well with Peck's belief in the existence of a collective unconscious.

> [W]e think, "God is as God was and always will be." But it's not the way I think anymore. It's also hardly what the Bible suggests. . . . All life is in process. And since I choose to have a living God, I believe that my God is also in process."[76]

Many people who read Peck's books or hear him speak never fully comprehend what he is saying about God. As Wendy Kaminer, author of *I'm Dysfunctional, You're Dysfunctional,* puts it, "Even Peck's most avid readers would probably have trouble explaining his ideas."[77] This may be because when it comes to identifying God, Peck habitually makes comments that are seemingly contradictory.

For example, Peck usually describes God as a personal being; one that loves, guides and calls us. On the other hand, he often speaks as if God is an impersonal force. Sometimes Peck defines God in masculine terms. In other instances, however, he uses either fully feminine terminology or refers to God as a "He/She." (*Note the chart on the following page.*)

Peck only adds to this confusion by stating that God is actually neither male nor female when he says, "Not that He is male, not that She is female—He/She is both and more—but that He is after us, that He wants us, that He loves us beyond belief, and that He intends to have us, no matter how fast and far we flee."[78]

Personal God

"As a Christian, I believe that God calls us human beings . . . to certain, often very specific activities. . . . What God is calling me to do is not at all necessarily what God is calling you to do."[79]

"[U]nconditional love does not come as naturally to human beings as to God. . . . God unconditionally loves you and me and every other single person in the world."[80]

"Then there is the relationship between Jesus and God, so different in flavor from that of the Old Testament prophets to God."[81]

Impersonal God

"We do not have to make the journey alone. We can ask help of the force in our lives that we recognize to be greater than we are. A force that we all see differently, but of whose presence most of us are aware."[82]

". . . I am being manipulated by a power beyond me. . . . I choose to cooperate with it. . . . [T]his manipulative power is infinitely more intelligent than I am and seems to have my best interests at heart."[83]

"But God—or life—can speak to us in many ways."[84]

Masculine God

"God is not neuter. He is exploding with life and love. . . . I subjectively experience His reality as more masculine than feminine."[85]

"The reality is that God is the Bridegroom and that what He is saying to us is, 'Come to bed with me.' "[86]

When God, creating us in His own image, gave us free will, He had to allow us humans the option of evil."[87]

Masculine/Feminine God

"God loves variety; in variety he/she delights."[88]

". . . God resides both inside of us in His or Her still, small voice and, simultaneously, outside of us in all His or Her transcendent, magnificent otherness."[89]

"But God does not always speak. Often she is a 'silent God.' "[90]

On more than one occasion, Peck has spoken of God in even broader terms, admitting that when it comes right down to it, he really does not know who or what God is.

> God wants us to become Himself (or Herself or Itself).[91]

> . . . I believe that some of our drives, our intuitions, *do* come from God or from Whoever God is—something outside that is wiser, smarter than we are.[92]

> I do not pretend to know the true name of God. I see enormous virtue in the wording of the third step of AA and the other twelve step programs: "Make a decision to turn our will and our lives over to the care of God *as we understand Him*." I would only alter the phrase to "as we understand Him or Her."[93]

God, says Peck, is simply "too large to submit to any single adequate definition."[94] Consequently, like some other metaphysical subjects (e.g., prayer), God "has never been adequately defined. And never will be."[95]

Defining God can indeed be difficult, but Peck may be purposely making it more difficult than it has to be. Peck feels that the best place for someone to be in his or her search for spiritual truth is in a state of confusion.

Such a state is supposedly a blessing because "confusion leads to a search for clarification and with that search comes a great deal of learning."[96] As he puts it, one cannot "carve out a safe niche and hole up in it."[97] Even Jesus allegedly taught this.

> You know, when Jesus gave His big sermon, the first words out of His mouth were: "Blessed are the poor in spirit." There are a number of ways to translate "poor in spirit," but on an intellec-

tual level, the best translation is "confused."
Blessed are the confused. . . . Virtually all of the
evil in this world is committed by people who
are absolutely certain they know what they're
doing. It is not committed by people who think
of themselves as confused. It is not committed
by the poor in spirit.[98]

Confusion aside, there is at least one thing that Peck is
absolutely certain about when it comes to God—God is
definitely sexual. In fact, Peck frequently goes out of his
way to get this point across to his readers.

. . . I am indebted to the Episcopal theologian
and author Robert Capon for pointing out the
obvious logic that since God created us in His
own image, and since we are sexual creatures, it
might only stand to reason that God is a sexual
being. . . . This notion of God not only as a sexual being but as a particularly seductive one is
perhaps somewhat supportive of our traditional
masculine image of Him.[99]

Peck goes so far as to say that "sex and God are inherently connected."[100] Human sexuality and related issues
consistently appear in Peck's writings. Consequently, we
must look at his views regarding these delicate matters.
The following chapter not only explores Peck's views on
sexuality, but also examines his ethics and morals. As we
shall see, attitudes and practices he advocates are rarely, if
ever, thought of as Christian.

Endnotes

1. Miller, Russell. "The Road Warrior," *Life*, December, 1992, p. 74.

2. Kaminer, Wendy. *I'm Dysfunctional, You're Dysfunctional: The Recovery Movement and Other Self-Help Fashions* (Redding, MA: Addison-Wesley, 1992), p. 126; cf. "Psychiatrists Shouldn't Ignore Religion, Writer Says" by Mike McManus, *The Coloradoan*, August 1, 1992, p. B7 and "M. Scott Peck" by Diane Connors, *Omni*, October 1988, p. 125.

3. Kaminer, p. 129.

4. Peck, M. Scott. *Further Along the Road Less Traveled* (New York: Simon & Schuster, 1993), p. 171.

5. Peck, p. 107.

6. Peck, p. 107.

7. Peck, p. 107.

8. Peck, p. 107.

9. Peck, p. 108.

10. Peck, pp. 107–108.

11. Scheinin, Richard. "Author M. Scott Peck Challenges Our Notions of Love and Spiritual Growth," *San Jose Mercury News*, February 19, 1991, p. 8D.

12. Peck, M. Scott. *A Different Drum* (New York: Simon & Schuster, 1987), p. 45.

13. Peck, *Further*, p. 100.

14. Peck, *Further*, p. 103.

15. Peck, *Further*, p. 103.

16. Peck, *Further*, p. 104.

17. Peck, M. Scott. *A World Waiting to Be Born* (New York: Bantam, 1993), p. 21.

18. Elwell, Walter, ed. *Evangelical Dictionary of Theology* (Grand Rapids, MI: Baker Book House, 1984), p. 744.

19. Peck, *A World*, p. 21.

20. Peck, *A World*, p. 21.

21. Peck, *A World*, p. 78.

22. Sheff, David. "Playboy Interview: M. Scott Peck," *Playboy*, March 1992, p. 56.

23. Peck, *Further*, p. 154.

24. Connors, p. 129; cf. Sheff, p. 46 and Peck, *Further*, p. 160.

25. Connors, p. 129.

26. Sheff, p. 46.
27. Sheff, p. 46.
28. Sheff, p. 46.
29. Sheff, p. 46.
30. Peck, *Further*, p. 160.
31. Connors, p. 129.
32. Peck, *Further*, p. 160.
33. Connors, p. 129.
34. Peck, *A World*, p. 75.
35. Peck, *A World*, p. 75.
36. Peck, *A World*, p. 75; cf. Connors, p. 129.
37. Sheff, p. 51.
38. Peck, *Further*, p. 161.
39. Peck, *Further*, p. 161.
40. Peck, *Further*, p. 161.
41. Peck, *A World*, p. 249.
42. Peck, *A World*, pp. 86–87.
43. Patterson, Ben. "Is God a Psychotherapist?," *Christianity Today*, March 1, 1985, p. 22.
44. Patterson, p. 22.
45. Peck, M. Scott. *The Road Less Traveled* (New York: Simon & Schuster, 1978), p. 76.
46. Whitmyer, Claude, ed. *Mindfulness and Meaningful Work: Explorations in Right Livelihood* (Berkeley, CA: Parallax Press, 1994), p. 269.
47. Peck, *A Different Drum*, p. 298.
48. Peck, *A Different Drum*, p. 219.
49. Peck, *Further*, p. 206.
50. Peck, *A Different Drum*, p. 218.
51. Peck, M. Scott. *People of the Lie* (New York: Simon & Schuster, 1983), p. 205.
52. Peck, *People*, p. 104.
53. Peck, *A Different Drum*, p. 296.
54. Peck, *Further*, p. 169.
55. Elwell, p. 897.
56. Peck, *Further*, p. 169.
57. Peck, *Further*, p. 173.
58. Peck, *Further*, p. 173.
59. Peck, *Further*, p. 171.
60. Peck, *Further*, p. 171.

61. Peck, *People*, p.67.
62. Peck, *People*, p. 67.
63. Peck, *People*, p. 67.
64. Peck, *Further*, p. 171.
65. Peck, *People*, p. 67.
66. Peck, *Further*, p. 171.
67. Peck, *Further*, p. 18.
68. Peck, *Further*, p. 108.
69. Peck, *Further*, pp. 18-19.
70. Peck, *Further*, p. 18.
71. Peck, *Further*, p. 25.
72. Peck, *The Road*, p. 283.
73. Peck, *The Road*, p. 11.
74. Peck, *Further*, p. 25.
75. Peck, *A World*, p. 57.
76. Peck, *A World*, p. 297.
77. Kaminer, p. 127.
78. Peck, *Further*, p. 231.
79. Peck, *A World*, p. 61.
80. Peck, *A World*, pp. 56, 59.
81. Peck, *A World*, p. 58.
82. Peck, *Further*, p. 14.
83. Sheff, p. 54.
84. Peck, *A World*, p. 88.
85. Peck, *People*, p. 12.
86. Peck, *Further*, p. 98.
87. Peck, *People*, p. 78.
88. Peck, *A World*, p. 77; cf. Peck, *Further*, p. 173.
89. Peck, *Further*, p. 207.
90. Peck, *A World*, p. 89.
91. Peck, *The Road*, p. 270.
92. Sheff, p. 46.
93. Peck, *Further*, p. 234.
94. Peck, *Further*, p. 25–26.
95. Peck, *A World*, p. 82.
96. Peck, *Further*, p. 80.
97. Peck, *Further*, p. 80.
98. Peck, *Further*, pp. 80–81.
99. Peck, *Further*, pp. 230–231.
100. Sheff, p. 62.

CHAPTER 4
_____

Spirituality without Morality

*In a sense, what I have become is a highly successful
evangelist. I belong to a sort of hard-drinking, hard-
smoking, hard-swearing school of evangelism.*
—M. Scott Peck[1]

Buddhism was the first religious belief system embraced
by M. Scott Peck. As a Zen Buddhist, he no doubt had
access to various forms of Buddhist thought. Given his
ethical and moral standards, which this chapter explores,
Tibetan Buddhism seems to be the tradition that has significantly shaped his thinking.

According to Walt Anderson, author of *Open Secrets: A
Western Guide to Tibetan Buddhism*, the Tibetan Buddhist
ideal is to yield: "Go ahead and do it, whatever it is, if you
think you must and it doesn't harm somebody else. But pay
attention; be fully aware of what goes on in your mind and
body, of how it really feels."[2]

Especially significant is Peck's philosophy regarding the
blending of spirituality and sexuality. It reflects a heavy influence of Tibetan Buddhism, also known as Tantric Buddhism. The sexual philosophy of Tantric religions is linked
to several ideas. There is the belief that erotic love is a pro-

found experience that "opens the mind to a sense of awe and wonder akin to religious experience."[3]

Also present is the idea that during the act of intercourse, a transcending of boundaries occurs between participants, which leads to an experience of oneness with each other. There exists the additional notion that the best way to escape binding passion—in this case sexual lust—is to "go into the act that is desired rather than to retreat from it."[4]

Perhaps the most important part of Tantric religions, including Tibetan Buddhism, is the belief that male and female energies reside in everyone. The male energy is said to be the dynamic, powerful and moving force. The female energy is thought of as static and docile. These two energies correspond to aspects of one's spirituality.

The female side is connected to inward properties such as "wisdom and realization" and is linked to "the more symbolic or intuitive aspects of understanding."[5] The dynamic (male) side "relates to outgoing aspects such as compassion and strength," as well as cognitive knowledge.[6] The goal of Tantric sex practices is to unite these two spiritual forces through physical union. This seems to be the goal of M. Scott Peck's teachings as well.

The Joy of Spirituality

Peck believes that spirituality and sexuality are so closely related that the sexual urge actually rises out of our unconscious desire to reunite with the divine. He says that it is "an urge toward wholeness and a yearning for the godhead."[7]

Sex is essentially a spiritual experience, which is why "so many chase after it with a repetitive, desperate kind of abandon."[8] In other words, promiscuity is just a manifestation of one's search for God "whether they know it or not."[9] To support his theories about sex, he makes an observation some might consider rather crass.

Even atheists or agnostics, at the moment of orgasm, cry out, "Oh, my God!" or, "Oh Christ!" They may say, "I don't believe in God," but at the moment of ecstasy, or maybe at the moment of agony, they're yelling, "Oh God!"[10]

According to Peck, the entire sexual experience is "potentially religious."[11] Is a religious experience, then, potentially sexual? Of course it is, responds Peck.

It is no accident that throughout history most of the best erotic poetry has been written by monks and nuns. . . . God is a lover, as one theologian put it. Or as another put it, God is continually on the make—He/She is after our body and soul. There's something *terribly* sexual about it.[12]

In his 1991 novel *A Bed by the Window*, Peck attempts to portray this close relationship between sex and spirituality. Set in a nursing home, the book's story is described by *Life* magazine as "a blanket of graphic sex and murder."[13] *San Jose Mercury News* reporter Richard Scheinin notes that the novel is filled with "kinky material."[14]

For instance, one character in the story (the nursing home's deputy administrator, Roberta McAdams) "carries a whip in her briefcase and grows sexually aroused 'at the thought of discipline, at the word itself.' "[15]

At one point in Peck's bawdy tale, a nurse "performs fellatio on a spastic paralyzed 29-year-old, Stephen Solaris, with whom she has fallen in love."[16] The very next scene opens with a lecture on the Christian concept of grace.[17] It is no wonder that a *Los Angeles Times* book reviewer, in reference to *Bed by the Window*, wrote, "The sex in this novel made my hair curl."[18]

But Peck makes no excuses for his views on sexuality and spirituality. He says he can only agree with a friend's comment. " 'The sexual and the spiritual parts of our personality lie so close together that it is hardly possible to arouse one without arousing the other.' "[19] Peck's conclusion about spirituality and sexuality is almost predictable: "[I]n order to love God passionately, one has to be a passionate, sexual person."[20]

To reinforce how strongly he believes this, Peck shares the insights of yet another friend, a priest, who says that "[I]f a conversion occurs in a previously sexually repressed individual and is not accompanied by some kind of sexual awakening or blossoming, then he has reason to doubt the depth of the conversion."[21]

Peck maintains that the tremendous surge in sexuality after a *true* conversion is why there are so many "stories about ministers who become involved with female parishioners."[22] Of course, Christians and non-Christians alike usually frown upon such activity. Peck sees things differently. He takes a rather progressive view of marriage and extramarital sex.

Open Marriage

Peck offers little information regarding the actual identity and nature of marriage. Like God, marriage is simply "too large to submit to any single, adequate definition."[23] It cannot be defined simply as a relationship between two people because such a definition would not leave room for group or polygamous marriages.[24] Nor can marriage be defined as something between a man and woman. Peck asks, "If between a man and woman, where do long-term, committed homosexual relationships fit?"[25]

The best definition Peck can come up with for marriage is that it is "an organization of two people who have made a *commitment* to attempt to maintain the organization."[26] He also points out that at its best, "a long-term marriage [whomever it may involve] is a mystical sort of phenomenon, rich beyond description."[27]

Divorce, however, can be a good thing, too. Peck says

God can actually call us to it: "As I believe that God calls some to marriage, so I also believe that God calls some people to divorce. . . . [T]he only valid reason to divorce is that there is very clear evidence that that is exactly what God is calling you to. . . ."[28]

Two things are important to realize about the above comment. First, Peck is speaking of God as our own internal unconscious mind. In other words, if our internal wisdom or unconscious mind calls us to divorce, then it is a good and proper thing to do. Second, dissolving a marriage is not necessarily a terrible thing because marriage is not a commitment to another person, but only a commitment to the maintenance of an organization.

Peck understands that marriage is difficult work, and regularly reminds his readers that one's spouse is never going to meet all of their needs, especially their sexual needs. Hence, an extramarital relationship may be necessary on occasion. To Peck, an "open marriage" is really the only way to go.

> My work with couples has led me to the stark conclusion that open marriage is the only kind of mature marriage that is healthy and not seriously destructive to the spiritual health and growth of the individual partners.[29]

To support his contention, Peck cites and endorses the 1972 book *Open Marriage* by Nena and George O'Neill, which extols the virtues of an open marriage.[30] The advice contained in this volume sheds a great deal of light on how Peck feels about the relationship between a husband and wife. Noteworthy are the following comments made by the O'Neills.

- Monogamy, as our culture defines it, *is* closed marriage. It implies ownership, demands sexual exclusivity, and denies both equality and identity.[31]

- No one person can ever "own" another person . . . but the closed marriage contract creates the semblance of such ownership or possession, and the clauses of the contract are reinforced by our traditional cultural attitudes toward love and sex. The idea of sexually exclusive monogamy and possession of another breeds deep-rooted dependencies, infantile and childish emotions, and insecurities.[32]

- "Monogamy, then," writes Dr. Albert Ellis, "not only directly encourages the development of intense sexual jealousy, but also by falsely assuming that men and women can love only one member of the other sex at a time, and can only be sexually attracted to that one person, indirectly sows the seeds for even more violent displays of jealousy."[33]

- Man (and we mean both sexes) is not sexually monogamous by nature, evolution or force of habit. In all societies around the world in which he has been enjoined to become sexually monogamous . . . he has failed to live up to that standard. . . . [T]his human "failing" which we commonly call "infidelity" remains an extremely frequent occurrence. . . . [I]s it the "unfaithful" human being who is the failure, or is it the standard itself?[34]

- Sexual fidelity is the false god of closed marriage. . . . Sex in the closed marriage is envisioned in terms of fidelity, thus becoming the be-all and end-all of love. . . . In an open marriage . . . new possibilities for additional relationships exist, and open (as opposed to limited) love can expand to include others. . . . [Y]ou can come to know, enjoy and share comradeship with others of the opposite sex beside your mate. . . . These outside relationships may, of course, include sex. That is completely up to the partners involved.[35]

- Outside sexual experiences when they are in the context of a meaningful relationship may be rewarding and beneficial to an open marriage.[36]

Peck echoes these sentiments in declaring that it is possible "for some people, at least, to love more than one person at the same time, to simultaneously maintain a number of genuinely loving relationships. This itself is a problem for several reasons. One reason is the American or Western myth of romantic love. . . ."[37] Peck himself explains the thrust of his words.

[T]he myth, therefore, prescribes exclusivity for loving relationships, *most particularly sexual exclusivity*. . . . [T]here are some whose capacity to love is great enough for them to build loving relationships successfully within the family and still have energy left for additional relationships. For these the myth of exclusivity is not only patently false, but also represents an unnecessary limitation upon their capacity to give of themselves to others outside their family. . . . Joseph Fletcher, the Episcopalian theologian and author of *The New Morality* . . . reportedly said to a friend of mine, "Free love is an ideal. Unfortunately, it is an ideal of which very few of us are capable." What he meant was that very few of us have a capacity for self-discipline great enough to maintain constructive relationships that are genuinely loving both inside and outside the family [emphasis added].[38]

Perhaps the best summation of Peck's views on extramarital sex can be found in his 1993 book *Further Along the Road Less Traveled*. On page 227 he bluntly states that it is indeed possible for "extramarital sex to be quite chaste."[39] What does Peck mean by chaste? Chastity, he says, is "a three-way relationship between two human beings and God, in which God is allowed to call the shots."[40] In other words, we should let our unconscious mind (i.e., God) be our guide.

Free Love

Peck feels that premarital sex, commonly termed fornication, can also be "quite chaste."[41] In *The Road Less Traveled* he tells the story of how he helped a young female patient named Rachel realize that sex is *not* a matter of commitment. This enabled her to go out and experience the fullness of sex even though she was unmarried.

> She realized that sex was not a matter of commitment but one of self-expression and play and exploration and learning and joyful abandonment. . . . [S]he was free to allow her sexuality to burst forth. . . . Rachel had become a vivacious and openly passionate person who was busily enjoying all that human relationships have to offer.[42]

Peck's feelings about fornication also seem to have been influenced by *Open Marriage*, which states that "sex with love is best, but that doesn't necessarily mean that any other kind or degree of sexual involvement is wrong, debasing, or the result of neuroses."[43]

This controversial book additionally promises that "although good sex grows out of a good relationship, that is not to say that you can't enjoy sex with someone you only recently met. You can. . . . The idea that sex without love is destructive, alienating and unpleasurable is a purely cultural evaluation much akin to the idea that sex is dirty."[44]

Peck's views on sexuality are not even bridled by the professional ethics of his psychiatric profession. He confesses that he would have no problem engaging in sex with a patient if it would help their psychological or spiritual growth. "Were I ever to have a case in which I concluded after careful and judicious consideration that my patient's spiritual growth would be substantially furthered by our having sexual relations, I would proceed to have them."[45]

Such a position is especially disturbing when coupled with Peck's belief that all of us practice psychotherapy when we, out of genuine love, extend ourselves to nurture another person's spiritual growth (e.g., "our spouse, our parents, our children, our friends").[46]

An obvious question arises. If it is permissible for Peck to help someone by means of sex, would it be proper for us also to engage in sexual activity if we felt it would help the other person's spiritual growth? Apparently so, according to Peck. As he puts it:

> Since, as I have indicated, laymen can practice successful psychotherapy without great training as long as they are genuinely loving human beings, the remarks I have made concerning the practice of psychotherapy on one's friends and family do not apply solely to professional therapists; they apply to everyone.[47]

Peck's liberal attitude and ideas regarding sexuality extend even to children, whom he views as sexually aware even while still very young. "All healthy children experience sexual desire for the parent of the opposite sex," he writes. "This desire usually reaches its peak around the age of four or five and is referred to as the Oedipal dilemma."[48] He continues:

> The romantic love of the child for the parent is a hopeless love. The child will say to its parent, "I know you tell me that I can't have sex with you because I'm a child, but just look at how grown-up I am acting and you will change your mind." This grown-up act requires enormous energy, however, and ultimately cannot be sustained by the child. It becomes exhausted. Resolution of the dilemma finally occurs when the exhausted child accepts the reality that it is just

a child and cannot—and no longer desires to—pull off the appearance of adulthood. In so doing, the child also realizes it cannot have its cake and eat it too; it cannot both sexually possess its parent and at the same time be a child. It therefore opts for the advantages of being a child and renounces its premature sexuality. The Oedipal dilemma has been resolved. Everyone breathes a sigh of relief—particularly the child, who becomes visibly happier and more relaxed.[49]

With regard to the issue of homosexuality, Peck again takes a position not normally held by Christians. He believes, for instance, that there are some people whom "God created homosexual." Consequently, those who rigidly define homosexuality as sin, "do violence to the subtlety and complexity of God's creation."[50]

What about homosexuals in the church? Should homosexuals be ordained? There can be no blanket yes or no answer, says Peck. In fact, a similar question can be applied to heterosexuals. The bottom line is that it "depends on the homosexual. It depends on the heterosexual."[51]

Another sexual issue Peck has not hesitated to address is pornography. During a 1992 interview for *Playboy*, he commented, "I believe pornography *can* be healthy. Pornography can be used for good or for ill. . . . I think it's natural to look at pornography. *I* enjoy it."[52]

According to Peck, it is a false myth "that we should have no need to do such things as look at pornography."[53] With regard to the kinds of centerfolds he is most fond of, Peck expressed the following: "basically, the more provocative the better."[54] As the next few sections will show, pornography is not Peck's only vice.

"I Swear I'm A Christian"

Christians are known throughout the world as individuals who, because of their beliefs, avoid what has been termed as "rough language," or profanity. This especially holds true when it comes to using God's holy name in vain. Peck, however, is quite fond of swearing, as the following quotes indicate.

> I constantly tell people, "Look, I don't want to be your f—-ing Messiah."[55]

> Nihilism . . . assumes that there is no meaning [to life] and, consequently, it doesn't matter what the f—- you do.[56]

> Wherever I studied or worked, there was always some son of a b—— in charge whose guts I absolutely hated.[57]

Peck also uses God's name in vain without restraint or apology.

> I tell them I'm not interested in being a godd—n hero.[58]

> I don't want to be your godd—-ed messiah.[59]

How can Peck, as a Christian, justify such talk? He believes that Christians have a cockeyed understanding of blasphemy because they erroneously interpret the Second Commandment ("Thou shalt not take the name of the Lord thy God in vain") to mean "that you shouldn't swear or use dirty language."[60]

To Peck, blasphemy is

> using sweet religious language to cloak irreligious behavior. . . . [V]iolation of the Second [Commandment]—blasphemy—is the sin of

sins, the lie of lies. It is the pretense of piety . . .
the ultimate lack of integrity, the refusal even to
attempt to integrate one's behavior with one's
theology.[61]

Because Peck takes this view of profanity, he also has no
problem telling dirty jokes. For example, he regularly tells
one joke in particular involving a Christian woman and a
female prostitute parrot. One of the occasions on which he
told this joke was his March 1991 interview with *Playboy*.[62]

God's Addict

M. Scott Peck is an addict and makes no excuses for it. "I
must confess that I am an addict," he writes. "I am almost
hopelessly addicted to nicotine."[63] The truth of this statement is expressed by *Playboy* interviewer David Sheff who,
after his interview with Peck, humorously noted, "[Peck]
smoked so much that I felt as if the interview had short-
ened my life."[64]

Peck has other addictions as well. According to Dr.
Darvey Fuller, an oncologist at Valley Diagnostic in Har-
lingen, Texas, Peck "tends toward alcoholism."[65] This is
echoed by "Judy Andreas, a single mother in Suffern, N.Y.,
who carried on a correspondence and, she says, an affair
with Peck after seeking spiritual growth in one of his workshops in 1984."[66] " 'He was a drunk and a womanizer,' says
Andreas. 'What I found most reprehensible was his drink-
ing.' "[67]

These charges are not just rumors or examples of yellow
journalism. Peck himself admits to having some serious
problems. " 'People like me who like to drink,' he observes,
'could drink all day.' "[68] In *Further Along the Road Less
Traveled*, Peck also confesses, "[W]hile not quite addicted, I
happen to be partial to alcohol and other sedative drugs, all
of which are called central nervous system depressants. In
other words, I like downers."[69]

Interestingly, Peck does not feel that chemical addiction is inherently evil. In fact, there are actually some positive aspects to being an addict.

> It would be wrong to totally disregard the regressive aspects of addiction, but nonetheless, in working with people, I have found that the greatest payoff generally comes in emphasizing the positive. . . . emphasizing not the regressive aspects of the disorder but rather the progressive ones.[70]

What could be progressive, or positive, about chemical dependency? Peck says addicts have a terrible yearning to "go home," or back to Eden. Their most ardent desire—whether they know it or not—is to regain their lost oneness with the universe, their godhood. Consequently, "addicts are people who have a more powerful calling than most to the spirit, to God, but they simply have the directions of the journey mixed up."[71]

According to Peck, alcohol and drugs, like sexual promiscuity, are just manifestations of one's desire to return to godhood. This is why people are so comfortable at cocktail parties. Such experiences are momentary sensations of that lost oneness all of us crave to reexperience.

> [A] great deal of human psychopathology, including the abuse of drugs, arises out of the attempt to get back to Eden. At cocktail parties we tend to need at least that one drink to help diminish our self-consciousness, to diminish our shyness. . . . [I]f we get just the right amount of alcohol or just the right amount of pot or coke [cocaine] or some combination thereof . . . we may regain temporarily that lost sense of oneness with the universe.[72]

For anyone who would criticize him for his addictions, language and other shortcomings, Peck has an answer: "The work is more important than the man."[73] In other words, what he teaches is more important than how he actually lives his life. People should look to his words, not to his actions.

Concerning the specific problem of alcohol addiction, Peck justifies it to some degree by turning it into some sort of blessing.

> . . . God [our unconscious] deliberately created the disorder of alcoholism in order to create alcoholics, in order that these alcoholics might create AA, and thereby spearhead the community movement which is going to be the salvation not only of alcoholics and addicts but of us all.[74]

What exactly is the "community movement?" As the next chapter will show, it is nothing less than the most important aspect of Peck's teachings.

Endnotes

1. Dart, John. "Spiritual-Growth Evangelism: Path to World Peace?," *Los Angeles Times*, June 17, 1987, p. 4.

2. Anderson, Walt. *Open Secrets: A Western Guide to Tibetan Buddhism* (New York: Viking Press, 1979), p. 71.

3. Anderson, p. 62.

4. Anderson, p. 62.

5. Anderson, p. 63.

6. Anderson, p. 63.

7. Peck, *Further Along the Road Less Traveled* (New York: Simon & Schuster, 1993), p. 220.

8. Peck, *Further*, p. 220.

9. Peck, *Further*, p. 220.

10. Scheinin, Richard. "Author M. Scott Peck Challenges Our Notions of Love and Spiritual Growth," *San Jose Mercury News*, February 19, 1991, p. 1D; cf. Peck, *Further*, p. 220.

11. Peck, *Further*, p. 222.

12. Scheinin, p. 1D; cf. Peck, *Further*, p. 222.

13. Miller, Russell. "The Road Warrior," *Life*, December 1992, p. 73.

14. Scheinin, p. 1D.

15. Scheinin, p. 1D.

16. Scheinin, p. 1D.

17. Scheinin, p. 1D.

18. Sheff, David. "Playboy Interview: M. Scott Peck," *Playboy*, March 1992, p. 44.

19. Peck, *Further*, p. 225.

20. Peck, *Further*, p. 223.

21. Peck, *Further*, pp. 225–226.

22. Peck, *Further*, p. 226.

23. Peck, M. Scott. *A World Waiting to Be Born* (New York: Bantam, 1993), p. 95.

24. Peck, *A World*, p. 95.

25. Peck, *A World*, p. 95.

26. Peck, *A World*, pp. 134–135.

27. Peck, *A World*, p. 95.

28. Peck, *A World*, p. 136.

29. Peck, M. Scott. *The Road Less Traveled* (New York: Simon & Schuster, 1978), p. 93.

30. Peck, *The Road*, p. 93.

31. O'Neill, Nena and George O'Neill. *Open Marriage* (New York: M. Evans & Co., Inc., 1972), p. 246.

32. O'Neill and O'Neill, p. 240.

33. O'Neill and O'Neill, p. 246.

34. O'Neill and O'Neill, p. 245.

35. O'Neill and O'Neill, p. 256–57.

36. O'Neill and O'Neill, p. 257.

37. Peck, *The Road*, pp. 158–159.

38. Peck, *The Road*, pp. 158-159.

39. Peck, *Further*, p. 227.

40. Peck, *Further*, p. 227.

41. Peck, *Further*, p. 227.

42. Peck, *The Road*, p. 147.

43. O'Neill and O'Neill, p. 252.

44. O'Neill and O'Neill, p. 252.

45. Peck, *The Road*, p. 175.

46. Peck, *The Road*, p. 177.

47. Peck, *The Road*, p. 179.

48. Peck, M. Scott. *People of the Lie* (New York: Simon & Schuster, 1978), pp. 154–55.

49. Peck, *People*, p. 155.

50. Peck, *Further*, 104–105; cf. Peck, *A World*, p. 77.

51. Peck, *Further*, p. 105.

52. Sheff, p. 62.

53. Sheff, p. 62.

54. Sheff, p. 44.

55. Sheff, p. 44.

56. Sheff, p. 54.

57. Sheff, p. 58.

58. Connors, p. 132.

59. Brower, Montgomery. "Self-Help Guru M. Scott Peck Seeks the Road to Peace—For the World and Himself," *People*, October 26, 1987, p.127.

60. Peck, *Further*, pp. 210–211.

61. Peck, *Further*, p. 211.

62. Sheff, p. 44.

63. Peck, *Further*, p. 135.

64. Sheff, p. 44.

65. Miller, p. 79.

66. Miller, p. 79.

67. Miller, p. 79.

68. Miller, p. 74.

69. Peck, *Further*, pp. 135–36.

70. Peck, *Further*, pp. 138–39.

71. Peck, *Further*, p. 137.

72. Peck, *Further*, p. 19.

73. Miller, p. 79.

74. Peck, *Further*, p. 150.

CHAPTER 5

Community: Road to Planetary Salvation

> *In and through community lies the salvation of the world. Nothing is more important.*
>
> *—M. Scott Peck[1]*

In his 1987 book *The Different Drum*, M. Scott Peck makes a forboding observation: "The human race today stands at the brink of self-annihilation."[2] According to Peck, the only thing that can save us is something he calls community. "We must come into community with each other," he declares. "We need each other."[3]

Unfortunately, it is almost "impossible to describe community meaningfully to someone who has never experienced it—and most of us have never had an experience of true community."[4] Peck further asserts that there is simply "no adequate one-sentence definition of genuine community" because it is "something more than the sum of its parts. . . . Community, like a gem, is multifaceted, each facet a mere aspect of a whole that defies description."[5]

Despite the intangible nature of community, Peck manages not only to outline what community is, but also reveal what it is not. He further asserts that adhering to his teachings and rules about community is a must rather than an option: "For that is how the world will be saved."[6]

What the World Needs Now

When Peck uses the word "community," he is not necessarily referring to persons within a business, members of a church, residents of a city or people living in a neighborhood. What exactly, then, is "community"? It is "a group of people who have made a commitment to learn to communicate with each other with increasing depth, authenticity, honesty, and vulnerability."[7]

"Community" is comprised of individuals "whose relationships go deeper than their masks of composure, and who have developed some significant commitment to 'rejoice together, mourn together,' and to 'delight in each other, make others' conditions our own.' "[8]

When community emerges, people are "able to accept and transcend their differences regardless of the diversity of their backgrounds (social, spiritual, educational, ethnic, economic, political, etc.). This enables them to communicate effectively and openly and to work together toward goals identified as being for their common good."[9]

Peck says there are a number of benefits to community. For example, joy "is an uncapturable yet utterly predictable side effect of genuine community."[10] Those who achieve community also "share love, honesty, harmony, openness . . . set differences aside and work easily together."[11] In and through community, people "can communicate openly, deal with difficult issues, tolerate ambiguity, resolve conflict, and become effective workers, all by following a few simple rules."[12]

To illustrate community, Peck often points to a phenomenon that frequently occurs between people during crisis situations such as hurricanes, floods or other disasters. In these instances, "people tend to drop their pretenses, overcome obstacles and reach out to help or emotionally support one another and, in the process, find surprising strength, tolerance and acceptance."[13] There is an "allness" to community, explains Peck.

> It is not merely a matter of including different sexes, races, and creeds. It is also inclusive of the full range of human emotions. Tears are as welcome as laughter, fear as well as faith. And different styles: hawks and doves . . . the talkative and the silent. All human differences are included. All "soft" individuality is nurtured.[14]

Such togetherness is not confined to disasters. In fact, during his high school years is when Peck received his first taste of community.

> Despite the hardness of the wooden benches in the Quaker meetinghouse . . . all the boundaries between people were soft. . . . Friends Seminary created an atmosphere in which individualism flourished. . . . [W]e were in truth all "Friends." I remember no divisiveness; I remember much cohesiveness.[15]

Peck subsequently encountered a number of other life situations where community spontaneously happened. He wondered the obvious. Did community have to occur accidentally, or could it be consciously sought after and achieved? He received a positive answer through observing the well-known Twelve-Step program of Alcoholics Anonymous (AA), which Peck regards as "the most successful community in this nation" and possibly throughout the world.[16]

He notes that the great genius of alcoholics in AA "is that they refer to themselves as recovering alcoholics. They do not refer to themselves as recovered alcoholics or ex-alcoholics, but recovering alcoholics."[17] This is designed to remind the alcoholic that "the process of recovery is ongoing, the crisis is ongoing."[18] Hence, the all-accepting, loving and caring community of AA members is ongoing.

To Peck, the comfortability and willingness to "open up" that is present during AA meetings is classic community. The tolerance and nonjudgmental attitudes demonstrated by AA members is also indicative of the kind of mind-set Peck feels everyone should adopt.

Not everyone, however, is an alcoholic. Nor do catastrophic disasters last long enough for "community" to become anything more than a temporary diversion from "rugged individualism." To solve this dilemma, Peck began conducting workshops in the early 1980s on how to "get into community." Building community through workshops soon became "the cutting edge" of his life.[19]

This eventually led to the December 1984 formation by Peck and 10 others of the Foundation for Community Encouragement (FCE), a nonprofit educational foundation that "teaches the principles and values of community."[20] FCE—originally headquartered in Knoxville, Tennessee, but now based in Ridgefield, Connecticut—was formed "with the idea of incorporating A.A.'s way of thinking . . . with the goal of teaching individuals, groups and organizations to communicate, deal with difficult issues and overcome their differences to form communities."[21]

Although community-building can take place anywhere in the country (or the world), it does not happen quickly or cheaply. Each program takes at least two to three days of intense interaction between attendees. The standard program for groups numbering up to 50 people costs $1500.00 per day plus all traveling, food and lodging expenses for two facilitators, or group leaders, from FCE.[22] Achieving community is also something quite unnatural. Consequently, it demands rules that "must both be learned and followed."[23]

Building "Community"

FCE employs several techniques, or a "technology," designed to "intentionally assist groups in experiencing community."[24] These methods are pulled from a number of diverse sources: Christian monasticism, Quaker meetings, Alcoholics Anonymous and the Twelve Step programs, group psychotherapy and the work of management consultants.[25]

Participants in community workshops spend two or three full days "arguing, singing, praying, revealing dreams and reflecting in silence. Leaders direct them to 'be vulnerable,' 'embrace the painful as well as the pleasant' and start all statements with 'I.' "[26] Building genuine community "requires its members to honestly and openly speak their minds, to risk intimacy, to confess what is appropriate, to make the hidden known when doing so is helpful."[27]

The conversations that occur during community-making supposedly "dispel misunderstandings, bridge differences, unleash enormous positive energy and open new doors where there previously appeared to be only walls."[28] How far may this openness and honesty go? "Peck counsels simultaneous truth-telling and mutual respect for individual differences—up to the point at which an individual's behavior is destructive of community."[29]

> Through increased responsibility, risk, and vulnerability of its members a group develops into a "safe place"—providing an environment of acceptance, appreciation of human diversity, and nurturance of personal growth, healing and self-discovery.[30]

FCE's overall mission is to encourage people toward discovering "new and better ways of being together," which will hopefully enable individuals to accomplish several objectives: (1) to communicate with authenticity, (2) to deal with difficult issues, (3) to welcome and affirm diversity, (4) to bridge differences with integrity and (5) to relate with compassion and respect.[31]

> Community, as we [FCE] define it, is a way of relating to others that is mindful of who they are, their similarities and differences, and an awareness of the group as a whole—its dynamics and needs. It's a way of being with others, not just as an individual looking out for one's own agenda, but as a group member with responsibilities to and for the group. Finally, it's a way of aligning people, processes, and purpose.[32]

The bottom line of community-building seems to be that "if people understood each other better, they would get along better."[33] Both FCE and Peck realize that building community is not an easy thing to do. An FCE brochure reads, "Reaching community is both intentional and difficult. The group process requires that an individual give up learned defenses and habitual ways of behaving."[34] It requires "self examination of deeply held views about reality, and who other people really are. It also requires that group members trust each other and communicate honestly."[35]

Fortunately, those seeking to form community do not have to tackle the task alone. They are all taught to rely on "a Higher Power." This brings us to the more spiritual side of community.

The Unknown God

It has been previously mentioned that many of Peck's ideas about community are derived from AA despite the fact that most psychiatrists now view AA as merely a substitute addiction.[36] Peck disagrees forcefully. "[T]hat's a bunch of sh—," he exclaims. "A.A. works because it's a program of religious or spiritual conversion."[37]

The "conversion" to which Peck refers is found in the third step of AA and other Twelve-Step programs: " 'Make a decision to turn our will and our lives over to the care of God *as we understand Him*.' "[38] Acknowledging "God," or a "Higher Power" as it is sometimes called, is important to Peck because he believes we will never solve the personal and social messes we are in unless we first undergo "some kind of spiritual healing."[39]

This does not mean that Christian spiritual healing is needed.[40] As Peck states, "The solution lies in the opposite direction: in learning how to appreciate—yea, celebrate—individual cultural and religious differences and how to live with reconciliation in a pluralistic world."[41] Consequently, community-building mandates that everyone must "stop trying to convert, fix, or heal each other! It's not 'somebody fixing somebody else.' "[42]

Peck's way of thinking leaves no room for evangelism. "Live and let live" is his motto. In spiritual terms, it might be better said, "Believe and let believe." Exactly *what* one believes is relatively unimportant as long as the "something" that is believed in is conceptually higher than the self. This may be goodness, truth, love or "God" according to one's own understanding.[43]

Peck prefers the term "Higher Power" for two reasons. First, it is "simultaneously both more broad and more specific" than the term "God."[44] The term is more broad in that it is inclusive of atheists and agnostics. The term is more specific in that it points to something beyond us.[45] Second, "Higher Power" implies the appropriateness of submission of the human will "to something higher than itself."[46] This is said to help with motivation.

But even with the help of a Higher Power, you do not go from noncommunity to community overnight. In fact, four distinct stages eventually lead to community: (1) Pseudo-community, (2) Chaos, (3) Emptiness and finally (4) Community.[47]

The Pseudocommunity stage occurs when the group "attempts to purchase community cheaply by pretense. They are nice with one another but hide tensions and differences."[48] The Chaos stage comes in when the group "attempts to obliterate differences, not out of love but to make everyone normal."[49] Stage III—Emptiness—results when, "[A]fter feelings of failure, people empty themselves of suffering and pain."[50] Then comes the Community stage: " 'A kind of peace' develops as individuals allow themselves to be vulnerable. The atmosphere is lively and intense. 'The agony is greater but so is the joy.' "[51]

Peck concedes that not everyone can build community. Only the most spiritually advanced persons are courageous enough to let go of defenses, prejudices and old ways of thinking.[52] Such individuals are what Peck calls Stage IV people. They are the spiritually elite from whom people in stages I, II and III should learn.

Spirituality in Stages

Peck believes that the four stages of community development roughly correspond to the four stages of personal spiritual development. He came up with these stages after noticing some odd and seemingly inconsistent actions among the types of people he met throughout his life.

For example, religious people who came to him for counseling invariably left as atheists or agnostics. At the same time, atheists and agnostics who came to him would often end up deeply religious and spiritually sensitive. Peck soon realized that *"we are not all in the same place spiritually."*[53]

With this realization came another: "[T]here is a pattern of progression through identifiable stages in human spiritual life."[54] They are as follows: Stage I, chaotic/antisocial; Stage II, formal/institutional; Stage III, skeptic/individual; and Stage IV, mystic/communal.[55] Peck reveals that he himself has passed through all four and is in the final stage.[56]

Stage I

Stage I is comprised of nearly all young children "and perhaps one in five adults."[57] It is basically a place for those who are undeveloped spirituality. Adults in this category are Peck's "people of the lie," evildoers who "seem generally incapable of loving others."[58] Hence the term "antisocial." Stage I is "chaotic" because these same people are unprincipled and ruled by nothing but their own wills.[59]

People who remain stuck in this stage are those who usually end up either in jail, in some other form of social difficulty or dead through suicide.[60] Others, although they remain evil, rise to great positions of power. Such an individual may even become a leading political figure or religious guru. A few Stage I people actually make it out of their predicament and convert—so to speak—to Stage II.

Stage II

Stage II, the institutional stage, is a stage where one's vision of God "is almost entirely that of an external, transcendent Being."[61] According to Peck, these individuals may be better off than Stage I persons, but barely so. Their involvement in the church proper is hardly any different than a criminal's willingness to commit a crime after being released from prison just so he will be returned to jail, an "institution to govern him."[62]

Like someone enlisted in the military, Stage II people do little more than blindly follow the orders of an institution. The church runs their lives and gives them some sense of order, as opposed to the chaos in which they formerly lived.[63] Peck maintains that a significant characteristic of these individuals is their "attachment to the forms (as opposed to the essence) of their religion."[64] From this characteristic, Peck derives his label "formal/institutional."

Their vision of God "is that of a giant benevolent Cop in the Sky, because that is precisely the kind of God they need—just as they need a legalistic religion for their governance." Stage II people, or "fundamentalists/inerrantists," also "know or believe in the reality of evil. But they use the concept in very simple and destructive ways, and harbor harmful attitudes such as the following: 'Anyone who doesn't believe the way I do is possessed by the Devil.' "[65]

Stage III

The next stage of spiritual advancement, the skeptical/individual stage, includes all atheists, agnostics, skeptics and doubters. This may seem like an odd grouping of individuals for the next to last stage of enlightenment. But according to Peck, "[P]eople in Stage III are generally more spiritually developed than many content to remain in Stage II."[66]

Stage III people are "self-governing" human beings who are "no longer dependent on an institution for their governance."[67] They are "sophisticated and know that what is considered good in one culture can be bad in another."[68] They are "not the least bit antisocial . . . are often deeply involved in and committed to social causes. . . . They make loving, intensely dedicated parents. . . . Advance Stage III men and women are active truth seekers."[69]

It is when a Stage III person begins to get a glimpse of the "big picture" that he or she nears graduation to Stage IV, which Peck defines as "the mystic/communal stage of spiritual development."[70]

Stage IV

A person reaches Stage IV of spiritual advancement when he or she realizes the oneness of all things. Through the ages, writes Peck, "mystics of every shade of religious belief have spoken of unity, of an underlying connectedness between things: between men and women, between us and the other creatures and even inanimate matter as well, a fitting together according to an ordinarily invisible fabric underlying the cosmos."[71]

Peck illustrates this mystical mind-set by sharing a personal testimony about something that happened to him during a community experience (prior to his first book). The event took place over a weekend and involved a man whom Peck thoroughly disliked.

> . . . I suddenly saw my previously hated neighbor as myself. Smelling his dead cigar butts and hearing his guttural snoring, I was filled with utter distaste for him until that strange mystical moment when I saw myself sitting in his chair and realized he was the sleeping part of me and I the waking part of him. . . . More than connected, we were integral parts of the same unity.[72]

What Peck is describing as the earmark of Stage IV is nothing less than pantheistic monism, or the belief that all is one, one is all, God is all and we are God (see chapter 1). Pantheistic monism is foundational to the New Age movement. New Agers say we only *think* we are individual entities. Reality is that there is no "you-me" distinction. There is only one big "I."

This universal "I" includes not only every *person*, but also every *thing* (e.g., soil, wooden boards, raindrops). New Agers maintain that the ultimate state of consciousness occurs when individuality dissolves and is replaced by a recognition of our oneness with everything else, including God.

Pantheistic monism is not a new concept. It is a basic to Hinduism and can be found in a number of Hindu writings. For instance, references to Peck's notion of oneness can be found in the Upanishads. The idea of an "ordinarily invisible fabric"—Hindus call it Brahma—can also be found.

> There are, assuredly, two forms of Brahma [the one reality]: the formed and the formless. Now, that which is the formed is unreal; that which is the formless is real.[73]

This whole world is Brahma. Tranquil, let one worship It as that from which he came forth, as that into which he will be dissolved, as that in which he breathes.[74]

This final stage, says Peck, is "the most mature of the stages."[75] He further holds that it might be best to think of Stage IV as a "spirit of the law [stage], as opposed to Stage Two, which tends to be one of the letter of the law."[76] Remarks such as this one, as well as blatant attacks against Stage II "fundamentalists," are commonplace in Peck's writings.

Against the Church

Peck begins his 1993 national bestseller *Further Along the Road Less Traveled* with the admission that he is an evangelist. However, he quickly qualifies that statement.

An evangelist is the last thing on earth I ever thought I would become. . . . The word "evangelist" carries the worst possible associations and probably brings to your mind the image of a manicured and coiffed preacher in a two-thousand-dollar suit, his gold-ringed fingers gripping a leatherette-covered Bible as he shouts at the top of his lungs: "Save me, Jee-sus!" . . . I am using the word "evangelist" in its original sense—the bringer of good news.[77]

In a review of *Further Along the Road Less Traveled*, Matthew Scully, former speech writer for former Vice-President Dan Quayle, observes that it seems a slightly uncharitable remark for a Christian psychologist to make, especially one "whose vocation is to help us see through the surface of things . . . into each troubled heart."[78] Scully comments on other noteworthy passages in Peck's book.

The same dismissive tone recurs again and again, this rush to dissociate himself from those *other* Christians. Here one might expect the author to note that for all the Swaggarts and Bakkers he has in mind, there have been evangelists like John Wesley or Billy Graham. . . . But he [Peck] never does qualify these judgments. . . . Peck doesn't seem to mind at all if readers take away a false, simplistic, and unkind view of ordinary evangelists and the folks who make up their flocks—just so long as we all understand he's not one of them.[79]

As one reads through Peck's writings it appears that the nonjudgmental and tolerant Peck is in fact quite judgmental and intolerant of at least two things—orthodox Christians (inerrantists) and historic Christianity. He maintains, for example, that churches are an unlikely place to find community.

Towns are not, in any meaningful sense of the word, communities. And sight unseen, on the basis of my experience with many Christian churches in this country, I can be fairly confident that each of the churches in your hometown is not likely to be much of a community either.[80]

According to Peck, churches simply have a lack of, and thirst for, community.[81] In fact, "most parishioners can't even talk to each other about what is most important to them."[82] Community may also be absent from churches because they are allegedly filled with Stage I individuals (evil people): "Since the primary motive of the evil is disguise, one of the places evil people are most likely to be found is within the church."[83]

Peck believes that today's Christianity has deteriorated

into nothing but "magical hodgepodge."[84] Consequently, the church deserves to be blamed for a number of modern woes: "One reason for the Satanism that's running around today has been a tremendous hypocrisy and the failure of the Christian Church. . . . [In] the profile of the possessed person's character, we find somebody who's been screwed by the Christian Church, and they have good reason to hate the Church."[85]

Christianity is even partly responsible for the arms race and shares the blame for bringing humanity to the brink of destruction.

> The changes required to dismantle the arms race and to achieve world community are far more profound than revising an atlas. We are talking about a veritable revolution. Revolutions begin in the hearts and minds of the people. If they are to be peaceful, however, they must be facilitated by the peoples' institutions. Yet the two most significant and relevant institutions in this country—the Christian Church and the federal government—are seemingly impervious to change, unable or unwilling to incorporate the principles of community that would facilitate this revolution and save our skins. . . . The Church has sidestepped its responsibility to *deal* with the arms race.[86]

Peck's list of charges against Christians and Christianity are countless. The following is only a small sampling of them:

- Fundamentalists who do not want to hear Peck speak have not "preserved their passion for God and spirituality."87
- The modern church "has made a lie out of the expres-

sion the 'Body of Christ'. . . . Currently the Church is not only not the Body of Christ, it is not even a body, a community. It must become a community before it can serve as the Body of Christ."[88]

- "Most churchgoers practice superficial, inherited, hand-me-down kinds of religion, which—like hand-me-down clothes—may keep them warm but are still just trappings."[89]

- Most Bible-Belt residents have a "simplistic black-and-white religious faith that claims to have all the answers and doesn't deal with mystery."[90]

- Christians "(like alcoholics newly converted to AA, or criminals newly converted to a moral life) . . . *need* some very clear-cut, dogmatic kinds of faiths and beliefs and principles by which to live."[91]

- The sin of Christianity has been "the sin of practice—a failure to integrate its behavior with its theology."[92]

- "[M]any churchgoers avoid the issue of death like the plague. Most Christian denominations have even taken Jesus off the cross. . . . [T]hey say that they want to emphasize the Resurrection over the Crucifixion. But sometimes I can't help but wonder if they simply don't want to see all that blood and gore and the reality of that death in front of them to remind them of their own."[93]

Despite these broad statements, Peck ironically comments, "I am always leery of blanket ideas and concepts, because they tend to be simplistic and get people into trouble."[94] A thorough study of Peck's writings indicates that his rebukes of the Christian church may be partly due to the fact that Christianity is inherently an exclusivistic religion. In other words, Christians believe that salvation is possible only through Jesus Christ.

This is not what Peck believes. First, salvation to him is not entrance into heaven to be with God eternally. Salvation is the realization of one's own divinity (see chapter 3). Second, community cannot be achieved as long as someone believes that they have the corner on truth.

> Perhaps the greatest sin of the Christian church has been that particular brand of arrogance, or narcissism, that impels so many Christians to feel they have got God all sewn up and put in their back pocket. Those who think that they've got the whole truth and nothing but the truth, and that those other poor slobs who believe differently are necessarily not saved. . . . They don't realize the truth that God is bigger than their own theology.[95]

Peck has made it very clear on more than one occasion that the "great enemy of community is exclusivity."[96] One of the hallmarks of community is complete acceptance of another's differences, including religious differences.[97] Given Peck's negative view of Christianity and his openness to other religious belief systems, why does he continue to call himself a Christian? The answer is fairly simple—he has radically redefined the word "Christian."

Conversion or Diversion?

Peck now admits that after his supposed conversion in 1980, he still "didn't know yet" what it meant to be a Christian.[98] Soon after his "conversion," when he attempted to explain Christianity to an inquisitive patient of his, he could only remark that at the core of the Christian faith was some "strange concept of sacrifice."[99]

He has since adopted a tailor-made definition of Christianity based primarily on one line of a letter written by Saint Teresa of Lisieux (1873–1897): " 'If you are willing to serenely bear the trial of being displeasing to yourself [i.e., taking a reflective look at your shortcomings and failures], then you will be for Jesus a pleasant place of shelter.' "[100] Peck comments:

> [A] true Christian is anyone who is "for Jesus a pleasant place of shelter." There are hundreds of thousands who go to Christian churches every Sunday who are not the least bit willing to be displeasing to themselves . . . and who are not, therefore, for Jesus a pleasant place of shelter. Conversely, there are millions of Hindus, Buddhists, Muslims, Jews, atheists, and agnostics who are willing to bear that trial.[101]

According to Peck's definition, a Hindu, a Buddhist, a Muslim, a Jew, an agnostic and even an atheist can be a "Christian." This concept demonstrates yet another reason why Peck's writings and interviews are extremely confusing. He sometimes uses the word "Christian" to mean someone who holds historic orthodox Christian beliefs. At other times, he uses the word to mean *anyone*—regardless of their religious beliefs—willing to take an honest reflective look at themselves.

Given such a view, Peck understandably states that:

> any group of people (no matter what their religious persuasion or whether the word 'Jesus' is ever spoken) who are willing to practice the love, discipline, and sacrifice that are required for the spirit of community, that Jesus extolled and exemplified, will be gathered together in his name and he will be there.[102]

Again, Peck's language must be translated. He does not mean that Jesus is truly there in the community through the presence of the Holy Spirit. Instead, he means that Jesus is present figuratively: "The spirit of community, which is the spirit of peace and love, is also the spirit of Jesus."[103]

Words are very slippery vehicles for Peck. He excels at redefining and rearranging not only words, but sometimes even whole phrases. For instance, take the phrase "Jesus is my savior." Peck sees two different meanings to this phrase, depending on whether someone is a Stage II or a Stage IV person.

> At Stage II this is often translated into a Jesus who is a kind of fairy godmother who will rescue me whenever I get in trouble as long as I remember to call upon his name. . . . At Stage IV "Jesus is my savior" is translated as "Jesus, through his life and death, taught me the way I must follow for my salvation." Which is also true. Two totally different translations, two totally different meanings, but both of them true.[104]

Peck has revealed that his beliefs are actually a variety of Christianity, and that his particular variety "is not used to explain everything. It accepts and appreciates mystery."[105] Consequently, he maintains that it is perfectly acceptable to believe any of the world's religions, as long as you realize you still do not have all the answers.

> Wherever you might choose to anchor your spirituality—be it in Christianity, Judaism, Hinduism, Taoism, Buddhism, or Islam—you will have to accept these basic truths [e.g., loving your neighbor]. . . . Which religion that should be I cannot tell you, because each of us is unique.[106]

"God," asserts Peck, "unlike some organized religions, does not discriminate. As long as we reach out to Her, She will go the better part of the way to meet you. There are an infinite number of roads to reach God."[107] Peck is only echoing here the words of one of his spiritual heroes—Gandhi.

"Religions are different roads converging upon the same point. What does it matter that we take different roads as long as we reach the same goal?" And we are all struggling along the rocky, thorny road of the desert to reach God.[108]

Within Gandhi's thought, quoted in *Further Along the Road Less Traveled,* is contained the ultimate purpose of Peck's teachings—reaching godhood through any means, while at the same time being tolerant/accepting of the roads others are taking. This, says Peck, is the broad path to individual and planetary salvation.

Community is necessary because unless everyone achieves community, no one will have the freedom to do and believe whatever they need to do and believe in order to find their godhood. As *Publisher's Weekly* notes, Peck is arguing that "physical salvation and spiritual salvation no longer can be separated. . . . Peck foresees a new era of integration favorable to a community movement that calls for the universal application of the principles of tolerance and love."[109]

Peck hints at all of this in *The Road Less Traveled* when he warns that the individual's health "depends upon the health of the society; the health of the society depends upon the health of its individuals."[110] He has also said, "We can never become totally whole by ourselves—we are interdependent. Recognizing this is key to building intimacy and community."[111]

The entire essence of Peck's teachings, especially his thoughts on community, are perhaps best summed up by one line from *The Different Drum:* "I need you, and you need me, for salvation."[112]

Conclusion

According to M. Scott Peck, the Christian church is literally bursting with heresy. He defines heresy as something put forth "in the name of Christian doctrine but that seriously undermines what the doctrine is all about."[113] He makes an additional observation that is equally true.

> [T]he path to holiness lies in questioning everything. . . . I believe that before you undertake any adventure, and certainly any spiritual journey, you've got to know something about how to discern what is healthy and what is dangerous.[114]

I can think of no better way to start learning how to discern the difference between what is spiritually healthy from what is spiritually dangerous than with an in-depth comparison of Scripture and the teachings of M. Scott Peck. This shall be done in the following section by Dr. H. Wayne House.

Endnotes

1. Peck, M. Scott. *The Different Drum* (New York: Simon & Schuster, 1987), p. 17.

2. Peck, p. 17.

3. Peck, p. 17.

4. Peck, p. 17.

5. Peck, p. 60.

6. Peck, p. 21.

7. n.a., "The Small Group Letter: Scott Peck Talks About Our Barriers to Community and Intimacy in the Church," *Discipleship Journal*, July/August 1988, p. 41.

8. Peck, p. 59.

9. n.a., *Community Described* (FCE promotional literature), n.d., p. 1.

10. Peck, p. 40.

11. Miller, Russell. "The Road Warrior," *Life,* December 1992, p. 76.

12. n.a., *Your People Can Learn to Work Together* (FCE promotional literature), n.d., p. 6.

13. n.a., *Community Described*, p. 1.

14. Peck, pp. 61–62.

15. Peck, pp. 31, 32.

16. Peck, p. 77.

17. Peck, M. Scott. *Further Along the Road Less Traveled* (New York: Simon & Schuster, 1993), p. 146.

18. Peck, *Further*, p. 146.

19. Connors, Diane. "M. Scott Peck," *Omni*, October 1988, p. 132.

20. n.a., *Community Described*, p. 1.

21. Sheff, David. "Playboy Interview: M. Scott Peck," *Playboy*, March 1992, p. 50.

22. n.a., *Community Described*, p. 1.

23. Peck, *The Different Drum*, p. 21.

24. n.a., *Community Described*, p. 1.

25. Peck, M. Scott. *A World Waiting to Be Born* (New York: Bantam, 1993), p. 277.

26. Miller, p. 76.

27. Belis, Gary. "Beware the Touchy-Feely Business Book," *Fortune*, June 28, 1993, p. 147.

28. n.a., *Your People*, p. 5.

29. Harrison, James. "M. Scott Peck's Prescription: Healing in Community," *Christian Century*, January 6-13, 1988, p. 18.

30. n.a., *The Foundation for Community Encouragement*, (1995 Schedule of FCE Events), p. 5.

31. n.a., *Community Described*, p. 2.

32. n.a., *Your People*, p. 4.

33. Skow, John. "The Fairway Less Traveled," TIME, September 19, 1994, p. 91.

34. n.a., *The Foundation*, p. 5.

35. n.a., *Your People*, p. 5.

36. Peck, *Further*, p. 139; cf. Sheff, p. 50.

37. Sheff, p. 50.

38. Peck, *Further*, p. 234.

39. Peck, *The Different Drum*, p. 19.

40. Peck, *The Different Drum*, pp. 19–20.

41. Peck, *The Different Drum*, p. 20.

42. n.a., *Discipleship Journal*, p. 41.

43. Peck, *A World*, pp. 48, 90–91; cf. Peck, *The Different Drum*, p. 59 and Peck, *Further*, p. 36.

44. Peck, *A World*, p. 47.

45. Peck, *A World*, p. 48.

46. Peck, *A World*, p. 48.

47. Peck, *The Different Drum*, pp. 86–106.

48. Dart, John. "Spiritual-Growth Evangelism: Path to World Peace?," *Los Angeles Times*, June 17, 1987, p. 4.

49. Dart, p. 4; cf. Peck, *The Different Drum*, pp. 86–106.

50. Dart, p. 4; cf. Peck, *The Different Drum*, pp. 86–106.

51. Dart, p. 4; cf. Peck, *The Different Drum*, pp. 86–106.

52. Dart, p. 4; cf. Peck, *The Different Drum*, pp. 86–106.

53. Peck, *The Different Drum*, p. 188.

54. Peck, *The Different Drum*, p. 188.

55. Peck, *Further*, pp. 119–26.

56. Peck, *The Different Drum*, p. 188.

57. Peck, *The Different Drum*, p. 188.

58. Peck, *The Different Drum*, pp. 188–189.

59. Peck, *The Different Drum*, p. 189.

60. Peck, *The Different Drum*, p. 189.

61. Peck, *The Different Drum*, p. 190.

62. Peck, *The Different Drum*, pp. 189–190.

63. Peck, *The Different Drum*, pp. 189-190.

64. Peck, *The Different Drum*, p. 190.

65. Connors, p. 130.

66. Peck, *The Different Drum*, p. 191.

67. Peck, *The Different Drum*, p. 191.

68. Connors, p. 130.

69. Peck, *The Different Drum*, pp. 191–192.

70. Peck, *The Different Drum*, p. 192.

71. Peck, *The Different Drum*, p. 192.

72. Peck, *The Different Drum*, p. 192.

73. Hume, Robert Ernest, translator. *The Thirteen Principal Upanishads* (New York: Oxford University Press, 1931), "Maitri Upanishad," 6.3, p. 425.

74. Hume, "Chandogya Upanishad," 3.14.1, p. 209.

75. Peck, *Further*, p. 238.

76. Peck, *Further*, p. 238.

77. Peck, *Further*, p. 17.

78. Scully, Matthew. "Further Along the Road Less Traveled: The Unending Journey Towards Spiritual Growth," *The American Spectator*, March 1994, p. 74.

79. Scully, p. 74.

80. Peck, *The Different Drum*, p. 25.

81. Peck, *The Different Drum*, p. 57.

82. n.a., *Discipleship Journal*, p. 41.

83. Peck, M. Scott. *People of the Lie*, p. 76.

84. Sheff, p. 56.

85. Connors, p. 138.

86. Peck, *The Different Drum*, pp. 292, 300.

87. Peck, *Further*, p. 176.

88. Peck, *The Different Drum*, p. 300.

89. Peck, *Further*, p. 66.

90. Peck, *Further*, p. 176.

91. Peck, *Further*, p. 79.

92. Peck, *Further*, p. 200.

93. Peck, *Further*, p. 66.

94. Peck, *Further*, p. 41.

95. Peck, *Further*, p. 166.

96. Peck, *The Different Drum*, p. 61.

97. Connors, p. 132.

98. Peck, *Further*, p. 199.

99. Peck, *Further*, p. 199.

100. Peck, *People*, p. 11.

101. Peck, *People*, p. 11.

102. Peck, *The Different Drum*, p. 75.

103. Peck, *The Different Drum*, p. 76.

104. Peck, *The Different Drum*, p. 197.

105. Sheff, p. 56.

106. Peck, *Further*, p. 154.

107. Peck, *Further*, p. 155.

108. Peck, *Further*, p. 155.

109. n.a., "The Different Drum," *Publishers Weekly*, April 17, 1987, p. 58.

110. Peck, M. Scott. *The Road Less Traveled* (New York: Simon & Schuster, 1978), p. 166.

111. n.a., *Discipleship Journal*, p. 41.

112. Peck, *The Different Drum*, p. 17; cf. Connors, p. 125.

113. Peck, *Further*, p. 206.

114. Peck, *Further*, pp. 81, 204.

Part 2

Theology Meets
Dr. Peck

H. Wayne House

CHAPTER 6

Storming the City of God[1]

The Scott Peck gospel is an amalgam of psychiatry and Christianity, drizzled with Greek myth and Buddhism, cast in scientific jargon and the language of tough love, then larded with tales from his own life.

—Life, *December 1992*[2]

Who is M. Scott Peck? While Richard Abanes answered many aspects of this question earlier in this book, I have been asked in this second section to look deeper inside the ideas of this best-selling author and subject those views to the teachings of the Bible.

When I began reading Dr. Peck, I found myself intrigued by many of his concepts and captivated by his various case studies. I applaud his obvious concern for his patients and his criticism of psychotherapists who are cold and detached from the people they treat. His belief that people must take responsibility for their problems is also admirable.

Peck's manner of communicating his ideas is also appealing. He appears unassuming, honest and open, willing to listen and be taught. His non-clinical style of writing surely is one reason for his success. He does not sit in an ivory tower. He moves among the people.

Unfortunately, his theology is far afield from traditional Christian beliefs. His adherence to non-Christian, especially New Age, religious views is particularly evident in his later books. He says he admires the New Testament Gospels but later questions their accuracy and truthfulness. The Jesus he claims to love is a perversion of the One found in Scripture. Moreover, though he claims Jesus as Lord, there is no mention of Jesus as Savior. The necessary elements of salvation—the recognition of moral guilt, the need for a Redeemer from the condemnation of sin, the biblical sense of grace (quite different from Peck's view)—are nowhere developed in his works.

In short, he promotes a worldview that undermines any benefits his counseling may have to Christian and non-Christian alike. Moreover, he spreads confusion by labeling himself a Christian while at the same time denying every essential doctrine of Christianity. He has baptized his Freudian and Jungian theories, but a genuine conversion does not appear to have occurred.

Peck's response when asked about his Christian conversion requires us to read between the lines in hopes of seeing genuine biblical faith in Christ. His definition of a Christian—"anyone who is 'for Jesus a pleasant place of shelter' "[3]—hardly inspires confidence that he understands redemption and conversion as explained in the New Testament. This definition equally applies in Peck's eyes to Muslims, Buddhists and adherents of various other world religions.

At another time, when asked about being a Christian, he replied, "I don't like the term 'become a Christian.' I think we err in looking at things like conversion and salvation as though they are a one-time thing. . . . I believe we need to look at these things as ongoing processes. I hope to God that I'm going to continue to be converted until I die. . . ."[4]

In view of his responses, I am more concerned than ever about those subtle areas within his teaching which may lead the unwary reader down the wrong road. It is a road leading away from the city of God and toward the city of man.

Caution Signs

Reading Peck requires discernment, for he uses familiar Christian terms, but without their orthodox, historical meanings. "God" is not the transcendent being who is present in, but distinct from, His creation. "Sin" is not the rebellion of the creature against the laws of the Creator and Lawgiver, but the laziness of humans to move toward mental health. "Grace" is not God's undeserved favor toward His people, but the various benefits of life that come to those who make the necessary effort. "Love" is not the sacrificial expression toward other persons in which we seek their highest good, but the selfish desire to love ourselves so that we can love others. Each of these ideas will be explored in more detail in this and subsequent chapters.

Peck introduces a number of psychological concepts which have achieved common usage (such as the conscious and subconscious), then fills these terms with his particular brand of psychotherapy, picked up from Sigmund Freud and Carl Jung. He is also prone to "psychobabble"— using terms that are vague in meaning, confusing the reader as to what he is really saying.

In his letter to the Colossian Christians, a church besieged on every side by pagan perspectives, the Apostle Paul wrote these words: "See to it that no one takes you captive through hollow and deceptive philosophy, which depends on human tradition and the basic principles of this world rather than on Christ" (2:8).

Paul does not tell these Christians that all philosophy is in error. Rather he warns them to be on guard so that they will not be cheated of the wonderful things available in

Christ by giving heed to philosphical ideas that do not conform to Christ. We could easily use Paul's admonition and substitute the word *psychology* for the word *philosophy*.

Certainly not everything taught by psychologists and psychotherapists of the past and present are in error, yet much of it is contrary to the truth of Christ and His Word. Those who follow erroneous theories of psychology find themselves entangled in views that injure their spiritual and mental health, while separating them from the help found by practicing the truth.[5]

On the other hand, Dr. Peck does express a number of important concerns that must be addressed by the Christian—suffering, pain, salvation, wholeness and community—though the Christian will, I hope, interpret them much differently than Peck does. With discernment we may profit from Peck's writings (especially his illustrations and case studies), while recognizing the need to "contend for the faith that was once for all entrusted to the saints" (Jude 3).

What Map is Peck Using?

There are various philosophical, theological and scientific assumptions that Dr. Peck has made which cause him to adopt the positions he has taken:

His View of Scripture

"Life has no road signs"[6] expresses Peck's view that there is no one source to give guidance to us in this life. We must pull from different resources, constantly reevaluating their accuracy and adjusting our map of life accordingly.[7]

I believe his major weakness, especially since his announced embracing of Christianity, is his unwillingness to recognize the authority of Scripture over his life and work. The uniqueness, truthfulness and sufficiency of the Bible are either ignored or rejected outright. He finds truth outside God's special and general revelation, adopting a view properly called *syncretism*—the joining together of various philosophies and perspectives into a new philosophy. His own experience, Eastern philosophy and scientific psychology provide the sources for his thinking, along with the Bible—when, through the eyes of psychotherapy, it agrees with his other viewpoints.

When I see passages from the Bible interspersed (though sparsely) throughout Dr. Peck's books, I get the distinct impression that he has not taken the time to examine the text carefully and certainly has not put himself under the authority of God's Word. For example, the events of creation, such as the Fall, were considered by Jesus, Paul and their Jewish contemporaries to be historical occurrences,[8] but Peck dismisses them with the words, "The story of the Garden of Eden is, of course, a myth . . . [which explains] how we human beings evolved into consciousness."[9]

Though in an interview Peck said he read the Gospels, found them accurate and then fell in love with Christ, elsewhere he states, "I don't want to imply that the Gospels are totally accurate. Some things obviously seem to have been added. Others seem to me to be obviously missing."[10]

When confronted with the biblical teaching on homosexuality, hell or resurrection, he rejects each one. He has difficulty with Paul's teaching on homosexuality in Romans because "God created [them] homosexual."[11] The idea of a God punishing sinners in hell is repugnant: "I simply cannot accept the view of Hell in which God punishes people without hope and destroys souls without a chance for redemption. He/She wouldn't go to the trouble of creating souls, with all their complexity, just to fry them in the end."[12] Though he considers reincarnation possible,[13] "[o]n the other hand, I find distasteful the traditional idea of Christianity which preaches the resurrection of the body."[14]

The Bible speaks plainly on the areas with which Peck has problems:

- Homosexual acts are condemned both in the Hebrew and Christian Scriptures. Paul sees such sexual perversion as a sign of human debasement (Romans 1:26-27).

- Peck may have difficulty with God sending someone to hell, but the Bible provides ample testimony that this terrible place is real and that people, by the rejection of the truth of God, send themselves to hell (2 Peter 2:3-6).

- The biblical doctrine of the resurrection of the body is totally incompatible with the concept of reincarnation. More importantly, this doctrine, logically, is required for our salvation. As Paul said, "For if the dead are not raised, then Christ has not been raised either. And if Christ has not been raised, your faith is futile; you are still in your sins" (1 Corinthians 15:16-17).

Dr. Peck picks and chooses those aspects of Christianity he finds helpful for his philosophy of life and rejects the others. He can do this because he does not accept absolute truth.

A Commitment to Relative Truth

Peck often speaks of truth and our need to find it. In his belief system, however, truth is a moving target. It is elusive since what is true for me may not be true for you. Our truths may be in direct contradiction to each other. Nevertheless, as we are bombarded with new information, we must change our maps to adjust to new reality, Peck says, as we are on the road of life.[15]

The problem with such an approach was illustrated for me on a trip I recently took from Salem, Oregon to Denver, Colorado. The map I used had all the information I needed to get to Denver, but it did not have details of the city. When I tried to take a direct route to my hotel, I discovered that the street I was on did not go straight through but was separated by a river. Having the right map to exactly where you want to go is very important, as I learned by being forced into a circuitous detour.

If our goal to is to know God and dwell with Him, we need to be sure we are on the right road and have a map that will unfailingly lead us to our final destination. Peck's maps have contradictory trails and signs, and though it will lead us to some god, it does not lead to the true God. The Scripture speaks of Jesus being *the* way, *the* truth and *the* life, not *a* way, *a* truth and *a* life (John 14:6). It also teaches that there is a broad way that leads to destruction and a narrow way that leads to life (Matthew 7:13-14). The Bible is plain that not just any truth that meets our needs will do and not just any road leads to life and to God (John 3:18; 8:42-47).

Peck speaks of dedication to truth but never really finds a true focus for truth. He speaks of truth as reality and our need to see the "reality of the world":

> The third tool of discipline or technique of dealing with the pain of problem-solving, which must continually be employed if our lives are to be healthy and our spirits are to grow, is dedication to the truth.[16]

He also says, though, that our view of the world must be broad and must be constantly revised.[17] He believes that "clinging to an outmoded view of reality is the basis for much mental illness."[18]

He sees dedication to the truth as "a life of continuous and never-ending stringent self-examination."[19] Based on Peck's own experience, though, this truth is very much a moving target for he has moved from a vague adherence to Hinduism and Buddhism (*The Road Less Traveled*) to a fervent belief in some form of Christianity (*People of the Lie*) to the embracing of New Age thought with all of its relativistic views of truth and morality (*The Different Drum*).

How does Peck account for the ability to accept these totally different worldviews at the same time?

> We have a situation in which human beings, who must deal with each other, have vastly different views as to the nature of reality, yet each one believes his or her own view to be the correct one since it is based on the microcosm of personal experience. . . . We are indeed like the three proverbial blind men, each in touch with only his particular piece of the elephant yet each claiming to know the nature of the whole beast.[20]

This agnostic attitude toward having certain knowledge does not square with the biblical teaching that God has not left humans blind. He revealed Himself to us in creation (Romans 1:18 ff), in His written Word and finally and perfectly in His Son (Hebrews 1:1-2). Moreover, we may come to truth through the logic that God has given us and careful investigation of the time-space world in which we live.

Knowledge Comes Only by Experience, Not by Authority Figures

Peck's emphasis on relative truth fits well with his perspective that our knowledge must be experienced to be real. He apparently does not trust knowledge taught by others or handed down by religious authority. Everyone must come up with his or her own truth and this only happens through personal experience.

> We begin by replacing the religion of our parents with the religion of science. We must rebel against and reject the religion of our parents, for inevitably their world view will be narrower than that of which we are capable if we take full advantage of our personal experience, including

our adult experience and the experience of an additional generation of human history. There is no such thing as a good hand-me-down religion. To be vital, to be the best of which we are capable, our religion must be a wholly personal one, forged entirely through the fire of our questioning and doubting in the crucible of our experience of reality.[21]

In line with this rejection of parental teaching is his argument that parents and religious training are the main culprits in giving teaching without offering proper role models. He declares that parents of persons who do not have mental health ". . . serve as undisciplined role models for their children. They are the 'Do as I say, not as I do' parents."[22] He continues: "One seldom sees patients, for instance, who are not basically healthier mentally than their parents. We know very well why people become mentally ill."[23]

Similarly Peck blames orthodox Christianity for the problems of many of his patients. He speaks deprecatingly of "Calvinistic dreariness"[24] and refers to the parents of a patient as a "rigid fundamentalist preacher and his equally rigid and fundamentalist wife."[25]

He views a God who has high standards for His creatures and judges Him as a "dangerous, cutthroat God,"[26] a malevolent force, a God who is eager to cut the throat of His patients and inflict punishment on them.[27]

Though Peck blames the woes of his patients on their inadequate parents, on the other hand he speaks well of his own parents, who properly reared him. He does not answer how, then, he could have had so many problems that he desperately needed psychotherapy.

If Peck's views are correct, and if the psychotherapist is a parent substitute, as he indicates, why then should we not simply reject his books and ideas too, for they would have a similar religious and philosophical impact on us? But Scripture teaches respect and honor for parents and acceptance of their teaching, if it accords with biblical revelation (not just any religion) in Deuteronomy 4:9-10, 6:6-9; Exodus 20:12, Proverbs 1:8-9, Ephesians 6:1-4 and elsewhere.

Evolution Brings Our Growth

To Dr. Peck, the theory of evolution serves as an important comparison to the spiritual evolution toward spiritual (mental) wholeness which is the thrust of his psychiatric practice as well as his book. Recognition of the need for this spiritual evolution is necessary for proper growth: "Since patients are not yet consciously willing or ready to recognize that the 'old self' and 'the way things used to be' are outdated, they are not aware that their depression is signaling that major change is required for successful and evolutionary adaptation."[28]

Speaking of spiritual evolution, Peck says:

> For the process of extending one's self is an evolutionary process. When one has successfully extended one's limits, one has then grown into a larger state of being. Thus the act of loving is an act of self-evolution even when the purpose of the act is someone else's growth. It is through reaching toward evolution that we evolve.[29]

Yet this evolution of the self is against the difficulties of our present predicament (remember the opening words of *The Road Less Traveled*: "Life is difficult"). In order to demonstrate the possibility of overcoming this obstacle, he speaks of progress against the laws of regression. Peck speaks of the second law of thermodynamics, or entropy, as an example of evolution being a miracle working against the laws of nature, even as spiritual growth struggles uphill against old paths and ideas to finally move a person toward spiritual competence. "I state that the process of evolution is a miracle, because insofar as it is a process of increasing organization and differentiation, it runs counter to natural law."[30] "But as in the case of physical evolution, the miracle is that this resistance is overcome. We do grow. Despite all that resists the process, we do become better human beings."[31] Peck is wrong. Some grow; some don't. Some become better; some don't.

The conundrum for Peck is his acceptance of spiritual evolution occurring all around us while the majority of humankind has not responded in love toward other human beings. He ruminates:

> Everywhere is war, corruption and pollution. How could one reasonably suggest the human race is spiritually progressing? Yet that is exactly what I suggest. Our very sense of disillusionment arises from the fact that we expect more of ourselves than our forebears did of themselves. Human behavior that we find repugnant and outrageous today was accepted as a matter of course yesteryear. A major focus of this book, for instance, has been on the responsibilities of parenthood for the spiritual nurture of children. This is hardly a radical theme today, but several centuries ago it was generally not even a human concern. While I find the average quality of present parenting appallingly poor, I have every reason [what reason?] to believe it far superior to that of just a few generations back.[32]

He then cites Roman law where a father had absolute control over his children, even to kill them. He alludes to the Middle Ages when children were sent into apprenticeship as early as seven.

Peck is myopic about what people are expecting of themselves and has historical shortsightedness, if not blindness. We have not somehow "come of age" in our days. The historical example of the much maligned and misrepresented

Puritans is a case in point,[33] and certainly better than the Roman law Peck cites. The Puritans demonstrated tremendous love for their children and spouses. They were not drab but enjoyed color, laughter, hard work and fellowship with friends. They also took seriously their commitment to purity before God.

Behaviors—often ludicrous behaviors—that we find acceptable today were not acceptable years ago; we have gone a step back. Is Peck totally blind to the great strides in Israel and the church in contrast to their contemporary societies? Could it be that the inevitable progress of each successive generation is not a truism? Rather than the evolution that Peck hopes for, there is instead regression in the world. The progress of humanity is dependent upon the acceptance of the revelation of God given to each culture through the history of the world.

He then speaks of love being the thing that moves us against entropy that would cause us to regress. But where does love come from? This force of evolution, as well as grace—where do they come from?[34] Peck finds love and grace coming from God, as he conceives Him: "To explain the miracles of grace and evolution we hypothesize the existence of a God who wants us to grow—a God who loves us. . . . And if we take it seriously, we are going to find that this simple notion of a loving God does not make for an easy philosophy."[35]

Certainly this is true outside Judeo-Christian beliefs, as we observe in Dr. Peck's embracing of Eastern mysticism.

Reality Is Mystical in Nature

Peck, probably due to his considerable exposure to Zen Buddhism, holds to both a monistic view of reality and a pantheistic idea of God. Monists believe that all reality is one and that what appears to be distinctions in objects in the world we observe and experience are actually merely an illusion. For example, though the glass of water you might drink, as well as the glass itself, appear to be different entities from you, in reality you only think that you, the glass and the water are different. Note Peck's words as he approvingly explains this philosophy:

> In describing the prolonged "oneness with the universe" associated with real love as compared to the momentary oneness of the orgasm, I used the words "mystical union." The most literal of mystics believe that our common perception of the universe as containing multitudes of discrete objects—stars, planets, trees, birds, houses, ourselves—all separated from one another by boundaries is a misperception, an illusion. . . . They [Hindus and Buddhists] and other mystics hold that true reality can be known only by experiencing the oneness through a giving up of ego boundaries.[36]

Though he does not directly advocate monism here he does seem to recognize it as a truth[37] and believes such thinking may be helpful in developing the most spiritual growth in love: "The people who know the most about such things [love] are those among the religious who are students of Mystery,"[38] a term that Peck uses generally to especially speak of Eastern thinkers who seek to be in harmony with the world around them, over against Christian thinkers who understand the Creator and creation to be separate.

As a direct corollary to belief in monism, Dr. Peck advocates pantheism, a view that understands God to be the universe and the universe to be God. That is to say, there is no ultimate distinction between God and His world. We are each then God and He us; this is also true, however, of plants, animals and inanimate objects.[39] God ultimately is not a loving, all-good, personal being who came into the world to suffer for us and our redemption. Rather, God and we are all one and we simply need to get in tune with that

135

truth so that God can work through us. Peck sees that as our unconsciousness working through our conscious self to bring about spiritual growth and health.[40]

Speaking of this perspective, Peck says humans have a tendency to conceptualize in terms of discrete entities, so that various objects around us have their own identities distinct from other objects.

> [W]e tend to be quite discomfited if our identities become mixed up or confused. As we have previously noted, Hindu and Buddhist thinkers believe our perception of discrete entities to be illusion, or maya, and modern physicists . . . are becoming increasingly aware of the limitations of our conceptual approach in terms of entities.[41]

He then advocates a slight variation of this monistic theory when he says, "I conceive of the boundaries of the individual as being marked by a most permeable membrane—a fence, if you will, instead of a wall; a fence through which, under which and over which other 'entities' may climb, crawl or flow."[42] Even with this difference from straight Buddhism, the implications are the same: We are part of one gigantic mind and ultimately part of God. Now all we must do is simply realize this for our proper mental health and spiritual growth. Christians understand spiritual growth to occur when we are in harmony with the teachings of God that require us to conduct our lives in ways that reflect the moral character of God. We do not, however, seek a blending of God and humanity; as humans we seek to emulate the God who is transcendent over us, not become Him.

Psychotherapy Is a Panacea

Dr. Peck does not approach the subject of spirituality and psychology without considerable influence from his training in psychology and his life experiences. Certainly each of us have similar influences as we seek to understand our world, but knowing what these presuppositions are will help us to know where an author is coming from in his or her arguments and explain where he or she ends up. Peck's psychological biases, as well as his views on God, reality and truth, color everything that he writes in his different books.

To Dr. Peck, the examination of oneself is the key to personal health and ultimately to the health and salvation of our planet.[43] Most of us know the maxim that an "unexamined life is not worth living," or have heard the famous statement of Athenian philosopher Socrates, "Know yourself." Certainly to look at ourselves is important to determine how we may live better, more productive lives, but there is considerable difference between Athens and Jerusalem, whether to "know ourselves" or to "know God." Only in truly knowing God can we come to see ourselves in light of Him, the imperfect seeking to conform to the perfect. Any counseling that is of lasting, if not eternal, value must be in light of the revelation of God to us, for He really knows us. Dr. Peck, however, appears to rely on science, not revelation, for his tools to help patients.

M. Scott Peck firmly believes that the tool of psychotherapy, when properly practiced by the therapist and received by the patients, is a panacea for the world's and individual's ills. With total discipline, promises Peck, "we can solve all problems."[44] He believes, as we observed in the first chapter, that the four tools of discipline are delaying of gratification, acceptance of responsibility, dedication to truth and balancing.[45] These are worthy virtues that Christians should emulate. The problem is that these lofty ideals are put through the siphon of Eastern philosophy and seasoned with what is purportedly the assured results of the scientific method.

Peck views psychotherapy as the most important means to achieve mental health. Other means are available, such as nonprofessionals relating in love, but therapy is an important shortcut to achieving mental health:

> Genuine psychotherapy is a legitimate shortcut to personal growth which is often ignored. . . . It is possible to build a house without hammer and nails, but the process is generally not efficient or desirable. Few carpenters will despair of their dependency on hammer and nails. Similarly, it is possible to achieve personal growth without employing psychotherapy, but often the task is unnecessarily tedious, lengthy and difficult. It generally makes sense to utilize available tools as a shortcut.[46]

Not just any therapy will do, however, for it requires a therapist who is willing to reach out in love and acceptance to his or her patient:

> We are now able to see the essential ingredient that makes psychotherapy effective and successful. It is not "unconditional positive regard," nor is it magical words, techniques or postures; it is human involvement and struggle. It is the willingness of the therapist to extend himself or herself for the purpose of nurturing the patient's growth—willingness to go out on a limb, to truly involve oneself at an emotional level in the relationship, to actually struggle with the patient and with oneself. In short, the essential ingredient of successful deep and meaningful psychotherapy is love.[47]

As important as it is to have a credentialed and trained professional counselor, in the final analysis it is not the credentials of the counselor but the love that is expressed toward the patient:

No matter how well credentialed and trained psychotherapists may be, if they cannot extend themselves through love to their patients, the results of their psychotherapeutic practice will be generally unsuccessful. Conversely, a totally uncredentialed and minimally trained lay therapist who exercises a great capacity to love will achieve psychotherapeutic results that equal those of the very best psychiatrists.[48]

If Peck is correct, are we to assume that most therapists, like him, "extend themselves through love to their patients"? Apparently not, for in *The Road Less Traveled* he indicates that most, unlike him, are cold and academic.

It is remarkable, almost incredible, that the voluminous professional literature in the West on the subject of psychotherapy ignores the issues of love. Hindu gurus frequently make no bones about the fact that their love is the source of their power. But the closest Western literature comes to the issue are those articles that attempt to analyze differences between successful and unsuccessful psychotherapists and usually end up mentioning such characteristics of successful psychotherapists as "warmth" and "empathy."[49]

If the therapist does not have the sufficient commitment to maintain the relationship, the healing will not occur.

However, if the therapist's commitment is sufficient, then usually—although not inevitably—the patient will respond sooner or later with a developing commitment of his or her own, a commitment to the therapist and to therapy itself. The point at which the patient begins to demonstrate this commitment is the turning point of therapy.[50]

Two problems present themselves in view of Dr. Peck's admission:

1. If so little psychotherapy is done in love, then why is so much of it supposedly successful?
2. Are the Hindu gurus involved with psychotherapy? If not, how does their love simply work without it?

Moreover, what do the Hindu gurus mean by love? Do they mean the same as Dr. Peck? He never really addresses these thorny problems in his books.

What causes therapy to be successful? Dr. Peck indicates it is a loving relationship of the psychotherapist with the patient and the reciprocity of the patient to the therapist. The majority of those patients who do not respond this way, he admits, never stay with the therapy to fulfill their potential. "They are content to be ordinary men and women and do not strive to be God."[51]

There does not appear to be the kind of consistency in psychotherapy to bring about the panacea that Dr. Peck envisions. So why are there such fantastic results with psychotherapy? There may not be! Some studies show that many get over their problems without therapy.[52]

Whatever the theological point or whatever the problem, Peck sees them all from a psychological viewpoint. The corruption of sin is a problem of mental health. Even the Roman Catholic doctrine of purgatory, adopted by Peck, is considered to be one big psychiatric hospital.[53]

Psychotherapy is Science

Peck has an exalted view of psychotherapy as being scientific. Since so many in the scientific and general population do not view psychology as true science like the natural sciences, Peck reveals that he is sensitive to this criticism:

> It is customary for other medical specialists to accuse psychiatrists of practicing an inexact and unscientific discipline. The fact of the matter, however, is that more is known about the causes of neurosis than is known about the vast majority of other human disorders. . . . It is possible to come to know exactly and precisely how, when, where and why an individual develops a particular neurotic symptom or behavior.[54]

Are psychology and psychotherapy really this exact? Do they measure up to the same kinds of standards as the natural sciences? The evidence is quite to the contrary. It is highly doubtful, for example, that psychiatrists know the exact reason, as Peck contends, for why a person has a particular behavior. Unlike bacteria under a microscope or stars in the heavens, humans have too many variables and influences on their attitudes and actions (not to mention their free will) to be predictable. The famous philosopher of science and Nobel laureate, Sir Karl Popper, observed years ago:

> [P]sychoanalysis and its derivatives are decidedly pseudoscientific. They lie in the same realm as astrology or Marxism, definitely separate from true science such as Einsteinian Relativity. This is because they can make no specific predictions that can be experimentally tested so as to be proven true or false.[55]

The Religion of Science

Along with mistakenly viewing psychotherapy as a true science, Peck also assumes that his concept of science is capable of approaching areas of investigation other than the physical universe and laws of nature to determine truth. He contrasts his "objective" discipline with what he views as the superstition and dogmatism of religion. In the same breath, though, he says that science has a religious dimension, the ability to speak of God, a view generally unheard of among scientists:

> So for mental health and spiritual growth we must develop our own personal religion and not rely on that of our parents. But what is this about a "religion of science"? Science is a religion because it is a world view of considerable complexity with a number of major tenets. . . . The essence of this discipline [science] is experience, so that we cannot consider ourselves to know something unless we have actually experienced it; while the discipline of scientific method begins with experience, simple experience is not to be trusted; to be trusted, experience must be repeatable, usually in the form of an experiment; moreover, the experience must be verifiable, in that other people must have the same experience under the same circumstances. . . . Science is a religion of skepticism. To escape from the microcosm of our childhood experience, from the microcosm of our culture and its dogmas, from the half truths our parents told us, it is essential that we be skeptical about what we think we have learned to date. It is the scientific attitude that enables us to transform our personal experience of the microcosm into a personal experience of the macrocosm. We must begin by becoming scientists.[56]

Is he really this naive? We can't know something unless we have experienced it? Really? What about moon land-ings, being killed, historical events, certain forms of disease and pain, etc.? There were no new Red Sea crossings for the people of Israel, yet faith and trust in the historical reality of that deliverance was expected of the people of God.

Though he is wrong about psychology being a pure science, he is certainly right when he indicates that science is a religion, at least since many scientists hold to their theories as if they were theological beliefs. Peck is hopeful that his fellow scientists will follow his lead since he has confidence that scientists can lead the world to spiritual growth.

> One thing to suggest that science as a religion represents an improvement, an evolutionary leap, over a number of other world views, is its international character. We speak of the worldwide scientific community. And it is beginning to approach a true community, to come considerably closer than the Catholic Church, which is probably the next closest thing to a true international brotherhood. Scientists of all lands are able, far better than most of the rest of us, to talk to each other. To some extent they have been successful in transcending the microcosm of their culture. To some extent they are becoming wise.[57]

The turf battles in the natural and social sciences would not seem to indicate a brotherhood of unique proportions any more than among various religious bodies. Scientists are constantly squabbling over theories, professional credit and other prized intellectual possessions. I doubt seriously whether scientists possess any greater wisdom than the average person on the street.

Dr. Peck has high hopes for the evolutionary leap of humankind as scientists and those committed to improved mental health work in concert to align their personal consciences with the universal unconscious reality. How he believes this can be done we will look at in the next chapter.

Endnotes

1. This is a reference to *The City of God* written by St. Augustine after he had been informed that Rome had been sacked. He referred to God's kingdom which cannot be overthrown.

2. Miller, Russell. "The Road Warrior," *Life* (December 1992), p. 74.

3. Peck, M. Scott. *People of the Lie* (New York: Simon & Schuster, 1983), p. 11.

4. n.a. "Scott Peck Speaks Out about the Church, Community, and Crystals," *The Door* (May-June 1990), p. 8. It is doubtful that Peck is understanding this ongoing process in the manner described in Roman Catholic teaching, in which the participation in the sacraments provides ongoing grace from God necessary for the maintenance of spiritual life.

5. For those interested in certain dangers of psychology, see Gary Almy and Carol Tharp Almy, *Addicted to Recovery* (Eugene, OR: Harvest House Publishers, 1994), and for a helpful introduction to various sides of the question on the integration of psychotherapy and Christianity, see Stanton L. Jones and Richard E. Butman, *Modern Psychotherapies* (Doroners Grove, IL: InterVarsity Press, 1991).

6. Peck, M. Scott. *Further Along the Road Less Traveled* (New York: Simon & Schuster, 1993), p. 13.

7. Peck, *Further,* pp. 44-45.

8. When Jesus quotes from the first chapter of Genesis in Matthew 19:4, He implied its historicity, and the Pharisees did not dispute it. Likewise, Paul speaks of Adam and Eve as historical in First Timothy 2:13-14 and elsewhere.

9. Peck, *Further,* p. 18.

10. Peck, *Further,* p. 161.

11. Peck, *Further,* p. 104.

12. Peck, *Further,* p. 171.

13. Peck, *Further,* pp. 168-169.

14. Peck, *Further,* pp. 168-169.

15. Peck, M. Scott. *The Road Less Traveled* (New York: Simon & Schuster, 1978), p. 44.

16. Peck, *The Road,* p. 44.

17. Peck, *The Road,* pp. 44-45.

18. Peck, *The Road*, p. 46.

19. Peck, *The Road*, p. 51.

20. Peck, *The Road*, pp. 192-193.

21. Peck, *The Road*, p. 194.

22. Peck, *The Road*, p. 194.

23. Peck, *The Road*, p. 237.

24. Peck, *The Road*, p. 159.

25. Peck, *The Road*, p. 187.

26. Peck, *The Road*, p. 188.

27. Peck, *The Road*, p. 188.

28. Peck, *The Road*, p. 71.

29. Peck, *The Road*, p. 82.

30. Peck, *The Road*, pp. 264-265.

31. Peck, *The Road*, p. 266.

32. Peck, *The Road*, p. 267

33. See Leland Ryken, *Worldly Saints: The Puritans as They Really Were* (Grand Rapids: Zondervan Publishing House, 1986) for an excellent and balanced look at the Puritans. This stands in stark contrast to Nathaniel Hawthorne's biased presentation of them in *The Scarlet Letter*. See David Powlison, "Integration or Inundation?" in *Power Religion: The Selling Out of the Evangelical Church?*, Michael Horton, ed. (Chicago: Moody Press, 1992), pp. 201-202 for the manner in which the Puritans dealt with counseling needs. They had an elaborate and compassionate system for helping people with disorders.

34. Peck, *The Road*, p. 268.

35. Peck, *The Road*, p. 269.

36. Peck, *The Road*, p. 96

37. Peck, *The Road*, p. 96.

38. Peck, *The Road*, p. 181.

38. Peck, *The Road*, p. 108. Peck continues: "I recognize the possibility that this conception may be a false one; that all matter, animate and inanimate, may possess spirit. The distinction of ourselves as humans being different from 'lower' animals and plants and from inanimate earth and rocks, is a manifestation of maya, or illusion, in the mystical frame of reference. There are levels of understanding. In this book I am dealing with love at a certain level. Unfortunately my skills of communicating are inadequate to encompass more than one level at a time or do more than provide an occasional glimpse of a level other than the one

on which I am communicating."

40. Peck, *The Road*, pp. 260-261.

41. Peck, *The Road*, p. 262.

42. Peck, *The Road*, p. 262.

43. Peck, *The Road*, p. 52; see also Peck, *The Different Drum* (New York: Simon & Schuster, 1987); and Peck, *Further Along the Road Less Traveled*.

44. Peck, *The Road*, p. 16.

45. Peck, *The Road*, p. 18.

46. Peck, *The Road*, pp. 56-67.

47. Peck, *The Road*, p. 173.

48. Peck, *The Road*, p. 175.

49. Peck, *The Road*, p. 173.

50. Peck, *The Road*, p. 147.

51. Peck, *The Road*, p. 180.

52. Passantino, Bob and Gretchen. "Can Psychotherapy Be Integrated with Christianity?" *Christian Research Journal*, Vol. 18, No. 1 (Summer, 1995): 19.

53. Peck, *Further*, p. 169.

54. Peck, *The Road*, p. 236.

55. Quoted in Gary Almy and Carol Tharp Almy, *Addicted to Recovery* (Eugene, OR: Harvest House Publishers, 1994), pp. 214-215. See the excellent discussion on the issue of psychology as science, Bob and Gretchen Passantino, "Psychology and the Church, (Part 1)," *Christian Research Journal*, Vol. 17, No. 3 (Winter, 1994), pp. 21-38.

56. Peck, *The Road*, pp. 194-195. J.P. Moreland explains the division that occurred in the mind of many people as to the validity of theology as knowledge: "According to the great theologian Saint Augustine (354-430), 'We must show our Scriptures not to be in conflict with whatever [our critics] can demonstrate about the nature of things from reliable sources. . . . ' Since the believer takes Christianity to be true and rational, and since Christianity makes claims about the way the world is and how it came to be, then in principle it is possible for competing claims to conflict with biblical revelation. Thus, the church has historically found that Augustine's advice is part of her mission to the world.

"Today, things have changed. For a number of reasons . . . believers and unbelievers alike have come to understand religion in general and Christianity in particular such that they cannot, even in principle, conflict with scientific or philosophical claims about the world. Supposedly, something about the very nature of religion isolates it from other dicsiplines of study, especially, science." J.P. Moreland, *Christianity and the Nature of Science* (Grand Rapids, Baker Book House, 1989), pp. 17-18. Quotation from Augustine is from *De genesi ad litteram* 1.2.1. Brackets his.

57. Peck, *The Road*, p. 196.

CHAPTER 7

Driving Down a Dead-End Road

*My commitment to Christianity is the most important
thing in my life and is, I hope, pervasive and total.*[1]

*There is a way that seems right to a man,
But its end is the way of death.*
(Proverbs 14:12, NKJV)

As I pointed out in the last chapter, *The Road Less Traveled* poses some excellent issues to be examined by the
Christian, and much of Dr. Peck's advice regarding orient-
ing one's life would prove beneficial for all of us. He dis-
cusses four secrets to being a person with perfect mental
health: discipline, love, religion and grace. Each of these
are certainly important aspects of having a full and spiritual life. His emphases on proper discipline, including accepting responsibility, delaying gratification, dedicating
ourselves to truth and developing balance in our lives are
good suggestions for every one of us. The importance of
love and grace are welcome additions to psychotherapy. I
encounter at least three difficulties, however, in Dr. Peck's
advice.

First, he confuses the proper goal in counseling. Improving mental health does not improve a person's spiritual health. This confusion between the mind and the spirit moves him into areas in which he is not prepared to give counsel. Peck says there is "no distinction between the mind and the spirit, and therefore between the process of achieving spiritual growth and achieving mental growth."[2] Non-Christians, as well as Christians, are capable of mental growth. But non-Christians are spiritually dead toward God. Peck's approach has several negative effects: Non-Christians may be lulled into apathy about spiritual matters since his view implies that all are somehow being saved through counseling. Moreover, Christians who follow Peck's advice may believe that when they solve mental disorders they are also growing spiritually. Last, he minimizes the sacrifice of Christ on the cross to satisfy the judgment of God[3] against sinners.

Second, Dr. Peck uses terms that he invests with meanings different from those that Christians are used to. The ideas of personal discipline, which incorporates the acceptance of responsibility, delayed gratification, dedication to truth and balance in one's life are admirable. His "love" and "grace" certainly sound like terms a Christian would use. However, Peck uses these words much differently than the Bible does. Love in the Scriptures requires sacrifice and selflessness, whereas Peck's love is selfish.[4] Grace in Scripture is God's unmerited favor through Christ's work for the undeserving sinner. To Peck grace is a gift that we earn that eventually will help us become God Himself.[5]

Third, as an evangelist of the good news of mental health,[6] he speaks of changing one's life in ways normally reserved for the transformation brought about by salvation through our trust in the power of God and in Christ's work on our behalf. But a life changed through the supernatural work of God does not fit into Peck's agenda. In an interview with Ben Patterson, Dr. Peck said, "It is always within our power to change our nature."[7] Such a weak view of the sinful nature of men and women is a basis for him to believe that he can help a patient solve all of his or her problems. The Scripture paints a totally different picture which we will look at in the next chapter. But for now, we specifically want to respond to the implications of Peck's statement. If we can change ourselves, then what need is there of the atonement of Christ? None, in Peck's view. The idea of Jesus as an atonement is the concept he favors least.[8] His theology of the cross is that Jesus served as an example of the way to salvation in His life and death. Jesus paved the way, so to speak, to show each of us how to save ourselves.[9]

Such a view of the atonement is foreign to the teachings of the New Testament. It is foreign to the typology of the sacrificial lamb of the Hebrew Scriptures. Though Peck does not directly deny the atonement, at the least he finds it not very helpful because he feels it compromises human responsibility.[10]

In contrast to Peck, our salvation in Christ deals with past guilt before God, the power of the Holy Spirit to improve our lives now and the certainty of a perfect life with God after death. Peck's gospel is a poor psychological substitute for the complete salvation that God offers.

Peck's viewpoints are not merely sub-Christian or non-Christian; they are anti-Christian. Someone might respond that these ideas were written before Peck became a Christian in 1980. I agree, but I can find no place where he retracts his earlier comments. Moreover, he includes many of the same ideas in subsequent books and interviews. His proclamation of the gospel of spiritual growth and wholeness through discipline falls considerably short of the biblical doctrine of salvation by grace through faith. M. Scott Peck preaches a different gospel (Galatians 1:6-10).

Though the presentation of Peck's material from *The Road Less Traveled* in the first chapter of Part 1 follows the order in which Peck wrote his book, I shall adopt a different order, addressing first his most egregious errors regarding love, religion and grace, and then proceeding to a discussion of his call to discipline.

What Is Love, and What Does It Cost?

Dr. Peck begins his section on love by declaring that the energy for discipline, the movement toward spiritual growth, is love.[11] Having said this he goes on to say, "One result of the mysterious nature of love is that no one has ever, to my knowledge, arrived at a truly satisfactory definition of love."[12] Although he does not believe there has ever been a truly satisfactory definition of love, he attempts his own: "I define love thus: The will to extend one's self for the purpose of nurturing one's own or another's spiritual growth."[13] Peck then completes this idea with a nebulous remark and a platitude:

> [T]his unitary definition of love includes self-love with love for the other. Since I am human and you are human, to love humans means to love myself as well as you. To be dedicated to human spiritual development is to be dedicated to the race of which we are a part, and this therefore means dedication to our own development as well as "theirs." Indeed, as has been pointed out, we are incapable of loving another unless we love ourselves, just as we are incapable of teaching children self-discipline unless we ourselves are self-disciplined. . . . We cannot be a source of strength unless we nurture our own strength.[14]

This may be a psychological way to describe love, but it falls far short of the biblical precepts and examples of love, to which we shall turn momentarily.

I heartily agree, however, that love is the key to any meaningful and lasting relationship, whether we speak of God or people.

Peck Distorts the Meaning of True Love

Dr. Peck performs a valuable service in differentiating

mere physical attraction (discussed in part one and which we will not deal with at length) from commitment to a person. After the "new" wears off, if there is not a deeper relationship, a bond, even the most physically attractive person will not hold our interest. On the other hand, if we only love those who appeal to us visually, the great doers of mercy such as Mother Teresa would fail to reach out in self-sacrifice toward the supposed "unlovable."

Though I appreciate much of Dr. Peck's insight on love, he has developed a distorted view of true love; he has turned love on its head. His first mistake is that he sees the end or goal of love as one's own spiritual growth. If the goal were someone else's growth, his viewpoint would be less objectionable. One of the best definitions I have seen for love is "to seek another person's highest good."

Peck's perspective of love misses much of the full-orbed biblical ideal which includes first of all, love for God; second, love for others; and last, love for ourselves. His view, however, centers first on loving self, then extending that love to others so we can build ourselves. He forgets that our major duty is to love God above all.

In discussing the nature and goal of love, he says,

> The only true end of love is spiritual growth. . . . The more I love, the longer I love, the larger I become. Genuine love is self-replenishing. The more I nurture the spiritual growth of others, the more my own spiritual growth is nurtured. I am a totally selfish human being. *I never do something for somebody else but that I do it for myself.* And as I grow through love, so grows my joy, ever more present, ever more constant.[emphasis added][15]

What Peck says surely does not apply to the Christian as he or she surrenders his or her life to God and seeks to let God's love, shed abroad in our hearts, flow to other people. How does such a description of love fit with Jesus' example of what loving one's neighbor is to be? Should we understand that the love and compassion that the Samaritan had for the Jewish person who was beaten and left for dead was because he expected something out of it for himself? Just the opposite was true. It was not a self-centered act at all. That is what makes it so special. The Samaritan's actions were out of compassion alone.[16] As such, they exemplified Jesus, the greatest Good Samaritan, who died for us while we were still sinners, and apart from any personal desires, gave Himself for us (Romans 5:8).

So then, Peck's idea of love may sound good on the surface but it is an inversion of the biblical view of love and leaves out important elements. I defined love above as "seeking another person's highest good," acting toward him or her in such a way that his or her best interests are at heart. Love is a duty, not an option, and our first duty is to God. Our first responsibility is to bring glory to God, to put His concerns above our own or anyone else's. Dr. Peck never speaks of this all-important issue.

Our First Duty of Love Is to God

When Jesus spoke of the greatest commandment, it was to love God with heart, mind, soul and body (Mark 12:30, Luke 10:27). This requires the total commitment of our total being to put His interests, as revealed in His Word, above our own. To love with our hearts is to commit our affections and desires in life. To love with our minds is to be surrendered to a proper and pure knowledge of Him rather than the false wisdom of this world. To love with our souls is to dedicate our life to His cause. "For whoever wants to save his life will lose it," Jesus said, "but whoever loses his life for me will find it" (Matthew 16:25). Last of all, we must commit our bodies to God. God is spirit but has created us as spiritual/physical beings who have the freedom to yield our arms, legs, eyes and other members of our bodies either to His service in purity or to debased causes.

It is important to note here that the Scriptures depict a perverse society as one in which people are lovers of self more than lovers of God. This is the ultimate and first sin, seeking to please ourselves—following our own ideas, desires and pleasures rather than following our duty to obey God's will for us.

Our Second Duty of Love Is to Others

Our second duty is to love other people. Peck believes that we are to do this, too, but for a different reason than the biblical reason, one more limited in scope. He remarks that "genuine love for a relatively few individuals is all that is within our power."[17]

This view does not agree with the biblical command of love which requires a much broader expression than Peck seems to allow. The Bible admonishes us to love our neighbor as ourselves. As the parable forcefully teaches, we owe love to all those whom God brings into our path that we have the means to assist. Moreover, the apostle John says we should love all our brothers and sisters in Christ (1 John 4:21).

Most Christians have been taught, and rightly so, that there are different words for love in the New Testament. The *eros*, or erotic, love is probably more of what Peck is speaking of when he talks of "falling in love." He does not distinguish other forms of love. Another form of love is family love, *storge*, which refers to the natural affection felt among family members. The primary words for love in the New Testament are *philia* and *agape*. The former speaks of a friendship type of love and is affected by how people respond to us. The latter speaks of love that is an act of our will, not of emotions per se.[18]

It is *agape* I address in this section, a love of commitment to another. Dr. Peck seems to address at least an aspect of *agape* love when speaking of the "willing" not "feeling" aspect of love: "The person who truly loves does so because of a decision to love. This person has made a commitment to be loving whether or not the loving feeling is present."[19]

He even seems to understand how love can extend to the love of enemies as taught in the Hebrew and Christian Scriptures alike (Deuteronomy 18; Matthew 5; Romans 12). But what Peck gives with one hand, he appears to take away with the other. Note the following two quotes:

> Love is not a feeling. . . . On the other hand, a genuinely loving individual will often take loving and constructive action toward a person he or she consciously dislikes, actually feeling no love toward the person at the time and perhaps even finding the person repugnant in some way.[20]
>
> To attempt to love someone who cannot benefit from your love with spiritual growth is to waste your energy, to cast your seed upon arid ground."[21]

Does this mean, then, that loving enemies has no value, or possibly, based on his previous words, we can love enemies as long as it somehow builds us up? I really don't know what to make of Dr. Peck's nebulous and contradictory statements.

Unfortunately, even though Peck says much about love and at times approaches aspects of *agape* love,[22] he does not seem to understand this heightened form of love, as illustrated in his willingness to allow patients to blame others for their problems or to divorce spouses that do not serve to promote their own "spiritual growth." The New Testament does not have a word for love that encourages pride, lack of commitment, anger or the blaming of others for one's own failures (as we shall see in chapter 10); Peck's love is *nonlove*.

Agape is the love of the Good Samaritan, the love of God for the world (John 3:16). It is the type of love which can cause a woman and man to continue to commit their lives together through thick and thin (Ephesians 5:22-33). Only this kind of love stands the test of time.

Though love is difficult to define, as Peck acknowledges, we may see it plainly in the *actions* expressed by this love, as given by the apostle Paul in First Corinthians 13, eloquently paraphrased by J.B. Phillips:

> This love of which I speak is slow to lose patience—it looks for a way of being constructive. It is not possessive: it is neither anxious to impress nor does it cherish inflated ideas of its own importance.
>
> Love has good manners and does not pursue selfish advantage. It is not touchy. It does not keep account of evil or gloat over the wickedness of other people. On the contrary, it shares the joy of those who live by the truth.
>
> Love knows no limit to its endurance, no end to its trust, no fading of its hope; it can outlast anything. Love never fails.[23]

Certainly none of us measures up to this expression of love at all times, but it is the standard against which we are judged and the goal toward which we reach.

Should a Christian Have Self-love?

For Peck, the ultimate reason that we are to love another person is because it benefits us; in other words, Peck's "love" is selfish at its center. Because of this, he does not view a willingness to sacrifice for the benefit of love to be love, but rather masochism:

> The issue of masochism highlights still another very major misconception about love—that it is self-sacrificing. . . . Whenever we think of ourselves as doing something *for* someone else, we are in some way denying our own responsibil-

ity. Whatever we do is done because we choose to do it, and we make that choice because it is the one that satisfies us the most. Whatever we do for someone else we do because it fulfills a need we have.[24]

It is at this point that Peck misunderstands genuine love more than anyplace else I have examined. Love to him is self-serving and sacrifice is masochism—the truth turned on its head. Part of the reason for the perversion here is that Peck's definition of sin is contrary to the Bible's. Sin to him is failing to selfishly assert ourselves toward others in order to create spiritual growth in ourselves and others. In brief (in the next chapter I will present his view of sin and evil more fully), he fails to see that the root of all sin is what he glorifies as love, namely, self-centeredness. Due to his confusion he has deceived himself, his patients and his readers. His perspective is probably also responsible for his moral relativism discussed in chapter 10.

We naturally love ourselves and are concerned about our own interests. When that interferes with the higher duty we have to love God and be in obedience to Him, then it is wrong. That is not love but selfishness and self-centeredness; it is sin. When our interests are paramount to the detriment of other people and their needs, then again we are exhibiting something short of love.

Love and responsibility are balanced in Scripture so that though we love all people, we have a hierarchy of responsibility in which love is expressed. We have a primary duty to family, to fellow believers and to God foremost. One cannot actively express love to everyone simultaneously or fulfill everyone's needs fully, but this does not mean we cannot love them. As God brings opportunities and we meet these challenges with the gifts and capabilities He gives us, we are loving.

It is proper for us to have love for ourselves as long as we do not place this above our God and the legitimate needs of our fellow humans. The worth we have is not something we have created ourselves, and thus we have no room to take pride in our abilities or to be prideful in anything else good that comes our way. God is the Giver of every perfect gift we receive (James 1:17). He is also our Creator. The fact that He created us and that we bear the image of God is the thing that is good about us. We have a duty to respect, maintain and develop ourselves as created beings with this image of God. Don Matzat puts the proper twist to the controversy:

> [E]very person possesses dignity and value as an image-bearer of God. From this bedrock evaluation we derive the dignity of work and the family. Not to view oneself as created in God's image is to create a defective personality in those arenas. . . . There is nothing unchristian or unscriptural about having a positive view of one's abilities, talents, personality traits, and so on, so long as we, as believers, acknowledge God as the giver of all good things. Even a Christian salesperson would never (or should never) introduce himself or herself by saying, "I know that you won't buy this car from me because I am a poor, miserable salesperson."[25]

Paul the apostle on several occasions spoke of his abilities, callings, gifts and sufferings, but always acknowledged in the midst of this: "by the grace of God I am what I am" (1 Corinthians 15:10).

In this sense I believe in self-love. From this basis, then, we are capable of loving. Unfortunately, when we do not, it is because of our sinfulness. Christians, however, have the working of the Holy Spirit in their lives to overcome this impediment.

On the relationship between love and sacrifice, Peck believes that true love is self-serving, even if it benefits others, and that sacrifice is not an expression of love but rather of masochism. This is outrageous thinking. Sacrifice is genuine willingness to set aside one's own desires and pleasures and reach out at personal expense to meet another's needs. This is surely what we should learn from the Good Samaritan's story, from the grave risks and even death endured by the apostles and many other Christians in ages past, from the courageous attempts of many people who hid Jewish people during the Nazi atrocities. It is most vividly illustrated in Jesus Christ, who shared equality with the God of the universe but was willing to enter into an existence of servanthood, even to the death on the cross (Philippians 2:1-7). This was not self-aggrandizement; this was sacrifice. This was genuine love in action, something that we are asked to emulate in our own lives (Philippians 2:12-18).

Spirituality versus Religiosity à la Peck

Since Dr. Peck has said he has become a Christian, one might think he has totally reoriented his life to match his new faith. Peck, however, seems not to be striving to be identified with traditional Christianity, but instead striving to blaze his own path. Part of the way he does this is by not using certain "religious" words so as not to corrupt "holy" words, ones that might be identified with organized religion.[26] He believes that so many have been harmed by religion that such terms might hinder spiritual growth.[27]

Moreover, having been baptized as a Christian does not cause him to believe that Christianity is more special or true than other religions—all religions teach the same truths, he thinks. Peck quotes the Dalai Lama to this effect: "Every major religion of the world has similar ideas of love, the same goal of benefiting humanity through spiritual practice, and the same effect of making their followers into better human beings."[28]

All Roads Lead to God

Though a Christian, Peck does not want to influence anyone toward any particular religion because all have the same truths, but one may fit one person better than another, since we are all unique.[29] In the words of Gandhi: "Religions are different roads converging upon the same point. What does it matter that we take different roads as long as we reach the same goal?"[30]

In response to Gandhi, Peck says God does not discriminate; the issue is whether we reach out to God:

> There are an infinite number of roads to reach God. People can come to God through alcoholism, they can come to God though Zen Buddhism, as I did, and they can come to God through the multiple "New Thought" Christian churches even though they are distinctly heretical. For all I know, they can come to God through Shirley MacLaine. People are at various stages of readiness, and when they're ready, virtually anything can speak to them.[31]

Peck's views are preposterous in light of New Testament teaching. All religions do *not* lead to God. The world in its wisdom does not know God (Romans 1:21). Peter insisted the name of Jesus alone can save. "There is no other name under heaven given to men by which we must be saved" (Acts 4:12). This religious inclusiveness is a delusion that has rested on Dr. Peck and those who think like him, and it is Satan blinding people from seeing the glorious light of Christ and being saved (2 Corinthians 4:4). Paul says that the Gentile Christians, prior to faith in Christ, were like their pagan counterparts, without Christ and without hope (see Ephesians 2:12).

Our Religious Views Are Inherited from Others

How do people usually become religious? Peck suggests

that it is through transference, namely, inheriting beliefs from our parents. How should we respond to our parents' teaching? He says we "must rebel against and reject the religion of our parents, for inevitably their world view will be narrower than that of which we are capable."[32]

What Peck is advocating may be appropriate if our parents adhere to false religions contrary to revealed truth in Scripture. If godly parents have passed on the true faith of Christianity (1 Timothy 3:15), then the proper response is to embrace the teaching and pass it on to our children (Deuteronomy 6:7-9, Jude 3).

What religion we are, then, is basically determined by the influences around us, according to Peck:

> If we are European we are likely to believe that Christ was a white man, and if we are African that he was a black man. If one is an Indian who was born and raised in Benares or Bombay, one is likely to become a Hindu and possess what has been described as a pessimistic world view. If one is an American born and raised in Indiana, one is more likely to become a Christian than a Hindu and to possess a somewhat more optimistic world view. We tend to believe what the people around us believe, and we tend to accept as truth what these people tell us of the nature of the world as we listen to them during our formative years.[33]

In order to attain mental health we must, he says, rid ourselves of our past views and look for new ideas in order to grow: "To develop a religion or world view that is realistic—that is, conforms to the reality of the cosmos and our role in it, as best we can know that reality—we must constantly revise and extend our understanding to include new knowledge of the larger world."[34]

For Peck, putting religions on an equal footing is virtuous, but claiming special knowledge about God is disturbing:

Those who think that they've got the whole truth and nothing but the truth, and that those other poor slobs who believe differently are necessarily not saved, as far as I'm concerned have a very small God. They don't realize the truth that God is bigger than their own theology. As I've said, God is not ours to possess, but we are His or Hers to be possessed by.[35]

In *The Road Less Traveled*, Dr. Peck encourages his patients to develop their own religions, different from their parents'. For some this would mean leaving beliefs in Christianity for atheism. For atheists, it might mean coming to a belief in God. The important thing for Peck is finding beliefs that meet the patients' needs. Observe his words:

So for mental health and spiritual growth we must develop our own personal religion and not rely on that of our parents. . . . To escape from the microcosm of our childhood experience, from the microcosm of our culture and its dogmas, from the half truths our parents told us, it is essential that we be skeptical about what we think we have learned to date. It is the scientific attitude that enables us to transform our personal experience of the microcosm into a personal experience of the macrocosm. We must begin by becoming scientists.[36]

Certainly people tend to adopt religious beliefs and practices from their parents and other influences in their lives. But so do they adopt various cultural attitudes and social graces. Why is it any more proper to rid oneself of religious beliefs than to throw off political parties or preferences for food? Moreover, the idea that Europeans adopted Christianity and Indians Hinduism does not account for the unparalleled growth of Christianity in the world. Whether in Asia or Africa, Christianity is growing faster than the birthrate. Surely the work of the Spirit of God to bring people to the knowledge of Jesus Christ must be taken into consideration.

In *The Road Less Traveled*, Peck lays out a four-stage development to spiritual growth (we will examine this in more depth in chapter 11). The first stage is for those who are "absent spiritually," having no use for religion. The second rung is for those who fit the description of the average Christian today, people who "envision God along the masculine model," who believe that God is a loving being and ascribe to Him a certain kind of punitive power.[37] State three is for skeptics, those who don't need church and "silly myths." The skeptics will reach state four if they continue on "the road." The last stage is for all the people "who have seen a kind of cohesion beneath the surface of things." These are the ones who throughout the centuries have spoken of "things in terms of unity and community." They are the ones who recognize and accept paradox and mystery.[38]

Where do those of us who are convinced of the historic Christian faith fit into Peck's categories? We are number two, not quite the worst but far below those who reject the teachings of our Lord Jesus Christ as they were delivered to His church through the apostolic writings.

Peck is religious without question, but what kind of religion does he adhere to? In the opening of this chapter I quoted from his second book in which he confesses his faith in Christ as the most important thing in his life. In his earlier book, written before his conversion, he expresses the need to move away from cherished beliefs in the past and reach toward a new religious experience through the help of science. Has he now left his old religion for the truth of Christianity? One would think so, but as the subsequent chapter will demonstrate, the acceptance of Christ has not materially altered his former beliefs. Christ appears to be merely another step in his spiritual growth toward the future.

That Peck's map leading to God is too vague and indescript to prove helpful is made clear by his approving statements of theologian Paul Tillich. Tillich's views of God are far different from those reflected in Scripture and historic Christian creeds:

> [T]here is reason to believe that behind spurious notions and false concepts of God there lies a reality that is God. This is what Paul Tillich meant when he referred to the "god beyond God" and why some sophisticated Christians used to proclaim joyfully, "God is dead. Long live God." Is it possible that the path of spiritual growth leads first out of superstition into agnosticism and then out of agnosticism toward an accurate knowledge of God?[39]

According to Peck it will take a sophisticated Christian to understand that declaring God to be dead is somehow the road to an "accurate knowledge of God." In chapter 9 we will look more fully at Dr. Peck's perspective of God.

Living a life in which there is no certainty, where the map is ever changing, does not sound like a cure for mental difficulties. It would bring constant unfullfillment and perpetual frustration.

Ruining a Good Song

The last section of *The Road Less Traveled* begins with a popular hymn, "Amazing Grace." This great and beautiful song sends a powerful message of God's wonderful favor on an undeserving sinner. This message, however, is obscured and distorted by Peck's understanding of grace. According to Peck, "[G]race is the ultimate source of the force [love] that pushes us to ascend the ladder of human evolution. . . ."[40]

Grace is

> . . . a powerful force originating outside of human consciousness which nurtures the spiritual growth of human beings. . . . [T]his force has been consistently recognized by the religious, who have applied to it the name of grace. And have sung its praise. "Amazing grace, how sweet the sound. . . ."[41]

In attempting to explain his concept of grace further, he says:

> Yet we cannot even locate this force. . . . Some of the phenomena we have discussed, such as dreams, suggest that grace resides in the unconscious mind of the individual. . . . The religious, who, of course, ascribe the origins of grace to God, believing it to be literally God's love, have through the ages had the same difficulty locating God.[42]

Grace, to Peck, is not the personal and loving work of God on the undeserving sinner, but a force that comes to us mysteriously and helps us along the road to spiritual growth. This grace may be in the form of accidental happenings in life, in dreams or through serendipitous events.[43]

Unlike biblical grace, which is totally unearned, Peck's grace is earned. He says, "Essentially, I have been saying that grace is earned. And I know this to be true."[44]

Peck interprets Jesus' words that "many are invited, but few are chosen" (Matthew 22:14) to mean that everyone is called by grace, but few are willing to listen to the call.

People receive this call, according to Peck, through their unconscious mind communicating with them.[45] It is because of this that patients are instructed repeatedly to say "*whatever* comes into their minds no matter how silly or insignificant it may initially seem."[46]

He speaks of Jung's theory of the "collective unconscious," "in which we inherit the wisdom of the experience of our ancestors without ourselves having the personal experience. . . . [W]e are actually only discovering something that existed in our self all along."[47] He continues, "Recent scientific experiments with genetic material in conjunction with the phenomenon of memory suggest that it is indeed possible to inherit knowledge, which is stored in the form of nucleic acid codes within cells."[48]

Dr. Peck is stretching his argument beyond reason. There is no evidence that specific facts and ideas that were in the minds of former generations are stored in genes and then through some osmosis are transmitted to us. The genes store knowledge, true, but only about the working of the human body—not the wisdom of the ages about philosophies, ideas, inventions, poems, medical cures, religious thoughts, etc.

Speaking of persons being accident-resistant, Peck writes, "Could it really be that the line in the song is true: 'Tis grace hath brought me safe thus far'?"[49] However, to Peck this is not the personal working of God as He, our Father, tenderly watches over us (Luke 12:22-34), but a mysterious series of beneficial events in our lives.

A person who has gone through psychotherapy may feel a kind of "rebirth" and "has no difficulty in understanding the words of the song: 'I once was lost, but now am found, was blind, but now I see.' "[50]

Certainly Peck is correct when he says his patients were lost; probably most really are. But the lostness is standing in rebellion to a holy God, separated from Him for all eternity unless they are graciously approached by Him. John Newton represents in the theology of his song "Amazing Grace" the very ideas that Peck repudiates and ridicules. Using this song of wretchedness and redemption for his purposes is absurd.

Peck has turned grace into an impersonal force which acts on our behalf to help us grow toward spiritual growth. The idea of grace in the Bible is integrally connected to God's undeserved favor bestowed on us wretched and rebellious sinners. This favor comes in the form of Jesus Christ's death on the cross, enduring the holy and righteous anger of God in our place. Peck still has not come to grips with the essential meaning of sin, dancing around it in *People of the Lie*. We will discuss Peck's idea of sin and evil in the next chapter and also look into the cross's importance to true Christianity.

Discipline: The Key to Spiritual Growth?

Let us now examine the road that Peck beckons us to follow toward discipline. It is here that I find most agreement with Dr. Peck, but even here there are serious errors to watch for as we navigate through the uncertain waters of Peck's theology.

Dr. Peck does not preach a gospel of redemption from sin through our belief in the work of Christ on the cross. According to Peck's "gospel" we can become spiritually whole through a system of disciplining our lives, loving ourselves and others and being receptive to grace. Through the first step of discipline "we can solve all problems."[51]

I agree with Dr. Peck that discipline is something sorely needed in everyone's life, Christian and non-Christian alike. I need more discipline in getting regular exercise and eating healthy food. Dr. Peck intimates that he needs greater discipline with an alcohol problem[52] and with chain smoking.[53] Being a more disciplined person is a worthy goal for each of us to reach, but exactly how we go about this becomes very important.

The holy Scriptures are a good place to start learning about spiritual growth. Paul tells us that the God-breathed Scriptures are profitable for being fully equipped for every good work (2 Timothy 3:16-17). Peter says that the promises of the Bible are adequate for "life and godliness" (2 Peter 1:3-4). Our Lord, in His High Priestly prayer to the Father, indicates how to be in proper relationship to God and consequently with others. We are sanctified through the Word of God (John 17:17). Paul additionally reveals that "faith comes from hearing the message, and the message is heard through the word of Christ" (Romans 10:17). From the Old Testament we receive excellent spiritual advice—to be careful whose counsel we take (see Psalm 1). People would do well to follow this advice in regard to the advice of Dr. Peck, as well-meaning as his advice may be, if it is contrary to the wisdom of God revealed in the Bible.

Peck sees the problems of life as a positive dimension of our lives,[54] and this certainly is in agreement with biblical texts and examples. The difficult trials of Joseph changed him from a young boy in need of some humility to a strong man of God who learned to resist temptation and temper justice with mercy and kindness (Genesis 36-37, 39-45). The trials of Job are well known. Job had wealth, power, family and health. Each of these was taken from him so that he would know that he was not responsible for the good things in his life. God was the Giver of gifts, and Job was only to be the grateful receiver.

The Scriptures teach this truth not only by examples, but by precept. "Who of you by worrying can add a single hour to his life?" (Matthew 6:27, Luke 12:25), asked Jesus. He taught that our efforts are to be in the power of God's strength and grace and not by our works. Much of my concern about Dr. Peck's ideas is the self-sufficient attitude rather than the "My grace is sufficient" perspective that God gave to Paul when he was discouraged about the thorn in his flesh (2 Corinthians 12:9).

Delayed Gratification

There is value in understanding Peck's perspective that we are to do difficult tasks now so that we relish the more pleasant ones later. I agree that the way to deal with life's difficulties is to confront problems square on with the anticipation of more pleasant experiences later. Most of us would rather put off painful confrontations or difficult jobs as long as possible.

The early church knew much about this, especially the martyrs. They could deny their faith for temporary relief, forfeiting the martyrs' crown, or they could face their persecutors, heads held high, embracing the joy to come. The entire Christian life is one of sacrificing the present in anticipation of our future glory with God. Peck's teaching has more temporal application, but the principle is the same.

Acceptance of Responsibility

Closely linked with dealing straightforwardly with life's problems is accepting responsibility for what we have done. Peck again sets forth a helpful concept when he says, "We cannot solve life's problems except by solving them."[55] He also wisely states that the "difficulty we have in accepting responsibility for our behavior lies in the desire to avoid the pain of the consequences of that behavior."[56]

Though there are many instances when other people create difficulties for us, we live in an age when people are willing to blame anyone besides themselves for their problems. We are a society of victims.

This is not new. To blame others was the first response of our distant forebears, Adam and Eve. Each of them blamed someone else for the sin (Genesis 3:11-14). This attitude is totally contrary to the biblical doctrine of confession, a word meaning "speaking along with." God says we are guilty of violating His laws, and in confession we freely admit this (1 John 1:9). Peck is right that we should not blame others for our difficulties or seek to excuse ourselves.

It is not so much what Dr. Peck says about responsibility but what he *doesn't* say that concerns me as a Christian. The Bible teaches that we are each responsible for our decisions in life and that we will be rewarded or punished for our deeds. On the other hand, the Scripture also teaches that we are to carry each other's burdens (Galatians 6:2). Also, we not only need to depend on others for help when we have problems, but we are to rely on the strength of God. None of us can be self-sufficient even if we are responsible for our wrong actions. Someone higher than we is needed to solve the problems of life. The Father is more than willing to meet our needs and help bear our loads because He is deeply concerned about us (1 Peter 5:7). The idea of "pulling ourselves up by our own bootstraps" present in Peck's solution is far short of the biblical ideal, partly because Peck does not believe in a personal God who cared enough for humanity to come into the world to atone for the sins of men and women. We cannot reform our lives without first being transformed by the grace of God and the power of the Spirit.

We now approach Dr. Peck's third key to discipline, where I believe he widely—and sadly—misses the mark.

Dedication to Truth

As I demonstrated in the previous chapter, Peck has a vaguely defined, evolving concept of truth. Certainly it is often true that one must abandon old ideas in order to discover new truth, but for Peck there is no way to find truth except by constantly altering the maps of life.

This idea is foreign to the Bible. God has revealed Himself and consequently His truth. It is the rejection of that truth, not its availability, that is humanity's dilemma. When Christ told His audience, "[Y]ou will know the truth, and the truth will set you free" (John 8:32), He set aside the "speculative" reality[57] of Peck. Not *a* truth or evolving truth, but *the* truth is what Jesus offers. The impact of knowing the truth is to be free. Jesus ties knowledge of truth with knowing Him, the very embodiment of truth. As in the garden, a decision must be made to know God and His goodness or to eat of the tree and know by experience the difference between following good and following evil.

To know truth one must be willing to accept it. Pilate's question, "What is truth?" (John 18:38) is never answered by Jesus. Jesus knew Pilate's heart and his lack of sincerity. Peck is in Pilate's shoes. Does he truly desire to know the true Jesus, the truth, or is Christ but one more experience (also tried) on his cosmic journey?

Jude says that he desires his readers "to contend for the faith that was once for all entrusted to the saints" (Jude 3), surely indicating a body of teaching held to be transtemporal.

We are to be no longer infants, tossed back and forth by the waves and blown here and there by every wind of teaching (Ephesians 4:14). Paul bases his whole eternity on the historical reality of the truth—Jesus rose physically from the dead—a truth Peck is not yet willing to acknowledge (see 1 Corinthians 15:3 ff).

Balance

I find Peck's discussion of balance a helpful presentation of an important subject, and one with which I largely agree with him. As discussed in the first part of the book, it is balance that provides the check on discipline. Each of us has many priorities which demand attention. Often we set them aside in favor of activities more pleasing (see section above on delaying gratification). In so doing, we fail others, God and ultimately even ourselves. It is very common to be rushed into the "urgent" affairs of life, while giving little time to those matters of real value, such as our families, exercise or time with God. Even Jesus once condemned the Pharisees for their many works while they failed in more important matters (Matthew 23:23-26). Christ is the perfect model of balance. He knew the right time to console and the proper time to rebuke. He knew when to mix with the crowds and when to retire to a private place. He knew when to demonstrate His power and when to slip away into the background. He knew when to avoid being taken by those who rejected

His message and when to surrender Himself to His ultimate destiny of the cross.

Balance is often exercised by giving up things, Peck indicates.[58] We must surrender some options to maintain a proper equilibrium between work and rest, food and exercise, expressing anger and suppressing it. As the Bible affirms, "There is a time for everything, and a season for every activity under heaven" (Ecclesiastes 3:1). On these points we share common ground with M. Scott Peck.

Endnotes

1. Peck, M. Scott. *People of the Lie* (New York: Simon & Schuster, 1983), p. 11.

2. Peck, M. Scott. *The Road Less Traveled* (New York: Simon & Schuster, 1978), p. 11.

3. He rejects the idea of a God who punishes humans. Peck, M. Scott. *Further Along the Road Less Traveled* (New York: Simon & Schuster, 1993), p. 171.

4. He seems to modify this a little in *Further,* where he seeks to distinguish between self-love and self-esteem. But I still believe he has not fully moved away from his earlier belief. It is difficult to know with Dr. Peck because he is willing to live with contradiction, and he expresses himself in vague terms.

5. P eck, *The Road,* pp. 282-283.

6. Peck, *Further,* p. 17; also see the review of *Further Along the Road Less Traveled* and *A World Waiting to Be Born* by Matthew Scully in *The American Spectator* (March 1994) p. 73-74.

7. Patterson, Ben. "Is God a Psychotherapist?" *Christianity Today* (March 1, 1985), p. 22.

8. Patterson, p. 22.

9. Patterson, p. 22.

10. Patterson, p. 22.

11. Peck, *The Road,* p. 81.

12. Peck, *The Road,* p. 81.

13. Peck, *The Road,* p. 81.

14. Peck, *The Road,* pp. 82-83.

15. Peck, *The Road,* p. 160.

16. See H. Wayne House, "Parable of the Good Samaritan and Its Implications for the Euthanasia Debate," *Issues in Law and Medicine* Vol. 11, No. 2 (Fall, 1995).

17. Peck, *The Road*, p. 119.

18. I recognize that, at times, the terms *philia* and *agape* may not be so distinct, but context reveals this. Generally writers do use the terms differently from each other with the meanings expressed here.

19. Peck, *The Road*, p. 119.

20. Peck, *The Road*, pp. 116-117.

21. Peck, *The Road*, p. 158.

22. "[B]y stating that it is when a couple fall out of love they may begin to really love I am also implying that real love does not have its roots in a feeling of love. To the contrary, real love often occurs in a context in which the feeling of love is lacking, when we act lovingly despite the fact that we don't feel loving." Peck, *The Road*, p. 88.

23. J.B. Phillips, translator. *The New Testament in Modern Enlgish* (New York: Macmillan, 1963), p. 371.

24. Peck, *The Road*, p. 115.

25. Matzat, Don. "A Better Way: Christ Is My Worth," *Power Religion: The Selling Out of the Evangelical Church?*, Michael Scott Horton, ed. (Chicago: Moody Press, 1992), p. 248.

26. Peck, *Further*, p. 211.

27. Peck, *Further*, p. 153.

28. Peck, *Further*, p. 154.

29. Peck, *Further*, p. 154.

30. Peck, *Further*, p. 155.

31. Peck, *Further*, p. 155.

32. Peck, *The Road*, p. 194.

33. Peck, *The Road*, p. 189.

34. Peck, *The Road*, p. 191.

35. Peck, *Further*, p. 166.

36. Peck, *The Road*, pp. 194-195.

37. Peck, *Further*, p. 123.

38. Peck, *Further*, p. 125.

39. Peck, *The Road*, p. 223.

40. Peck, *The Road*, p. 300.

41. Peck, *The Road*, p. 260.

42. Peck, *The Road*, p. 261.

43. Peck, *The Road*, pp. 253-259.

44. Peck, *The Road*, p. 306.

45. Peck, *The Road*, p. 245.

46. Peck, *The Road*, p. 245.

47. Peck, *The Road*, p. 252.

48. Peck, *The Road*, p. 252.

49. Peck, *The Road*, pp. 240-241.

50. Peck, *The Road*, p. 251.

51. Peck, *The Road*, p. 16.

52. Peck, *Further,* p. 135; Miller, Russell. "The Road Warrior," *Life,* December 1992, p. 73; and a statement by Peck made to Katie Couric on the "Today Show," October 19, 1993: "I don't think I'm an alcoholic, but I love my alcohol" as quoted in Fisher, G. Richard. "The Road Not Traveled: Unveiling the Bizarre Beliefs of M. Scott Peck," *The Quarterly Journal,* Vol. 14, No. 1 (January-March 1994), p. 1.

53. "Scott Peck Speaks Out about the Church, Community, and Crystals," *The Door* (May-June 1990), p. 14.

54. Peck, *The Road*, p. 16.

55. Peck, *The Road*, p. 32.

56. Peck, *The Road*, p. 42.

57. Patterson, p. 22.

58. Peck, *The Road*, p. 66.

CHAPTER 8

Dr. Peck Gets a Dose of Reality: The Problem of Evil

In Christian eschatology . . . there are two scenarios for Satan. In one all human souls, having been converted to light and love, reach out to the spirit of hate and falsehood in friendship. Finally realizing itself to be totally defeated . . . even Satan is converted.

—*M. Scott Peck*[1]

And the devil . . . was thrown into the lake of burning sulfur. . . . [and] will be tormented day and night for ever and ever.

Revelation 20:10

People of the Lie received much attention in Christian circles, establishing Peck as a "Christian" who boldly advanced the reality of sin, even though the word is taboo in the psychological community. He was seen as bold and daring to take a stand on this issue.

Also in *People of the Lie*, we first see the "Christian" Peck. He says in his most recent book, *Further Along the Road Less*

Traveled, that it was what he understood to be the Christian doctrine of sin that eventually led him to Christianity:

> One of the reasons I very gradually gravitated toward Christianity is that I came to believe that Christian doctrine has the most correct understanding of the nature of sin. It is a paradoxical, multidimensional understanding, and the first side of the paradox is that Christianity holds that we are all sinners. We cannot not sin.[2]

Peck explains what he is doing in *People of the Lie*. In acknowledging our sin-proneness, he largely seeks to examine "the very darkest members of our human community—those I frankly judge to be evil,"[3] Although he recognizes that each of us has a dark side, Peck has taken the right steps to recognize his inability to save himself and see the need of the Savior.

In spite of all the bravado, however, Peck has made only a partial trip to the biblical teaching on sin. He does not see the human race under the guilt of sin and God's just condemnation, nor does he have a theology of the cross that is consistent with what is emphasized in the writings of Paul and has been held by the church from its inception (Acts 2:22-24, 1 Corinthians 15:3-4). What appeared to be a change of direction in *People of the Lie* seems to be nothing more than a rest stop for Peck, at which point he then continues down the same wrong road he had begun, away from the kingdom of God.

What Is Sin in Peck's Worldview?

The biblical doctrine of sin is simple to understand but difficult to come to grips with in our lives. Sin is rebellion! It is setting our will above the will of our Sovereign Creator. Whether it is by violating specific laws He has given us (sins of commission) or failing to do what we know He has asked us to do (sins of omission), when we sin we decide we are in control of our lives and God is not. The Scripture uses a straightforward definition: "[S]in is lawlessness" (1 John 3:4).

Peck views sin altogether differently. Sin, in Peck's view, is what keeps each of us from achieving our godhood, from being God Himself. The goal of each person is to be released from emotional illness or from our lostness, our sinfulness, and set free to achieve mental health—our "salvation"—to allow grace to work in us. Peck says, "I have said that the attempt to avoid legitimate suffering lies at the root of all emotional illness."[4] Unfortunately, he could not quite figure out the problem that caused this avoidance. He believes that he found it in his doctrine of sin, the only thing that is keeping us from reaching our divinity: "Ultimately there is only the one impediment, and that is laziness."[5]

He characterizes his thinking in past years:

> For many years I found the notion of original sin meaningless, even objectionable. Sexuality did not strike me as particularly sinful. Nor my various other appetites. I would quite frequently indulge myself by overeating an excellent meal, and while I might suffer pangs of indigestion, I certainly did not suffer any pangs of guilt. I perceived sin in the world: cheating, prejudice, torture, brutality. But I failed to perceive any inherent sinfulness in infants, nor could I find it rational to believe that young children were cursed because their ancestors had eaten from the fruit of the tree of the knowledge of good and evil. Gradually, however, I became increasingly aware of the ubiquitous nature of laziness. In the struggle to help my patients grow, I found that my chief enemy was invariably their

laziness. . . . It was at this point that the serpent-and-the-apple story suddenly made sense.[6]

This psychological attempt to account for spiritual problems of humankind is a feeble effort to explain the nature of sin and the means to rid ourselves of sin. I shall develop more fully the biblical doctrine of sin in a moment, as well as provide the only real solution to the problem of sin.

How Dr. Peck Believes Sin Entered the World

Dr. Peck develops a scenario to explain the event of the fall, though the reader must understand that he does not believe Adam and Eve were real persons (see chapters 6 and 7); they are symbols of the dilemma that humans are in. Generally Christians have believed that the failure of this first pair was their disobedience to the expressed command of God not to eat of the tree of the knowledge of good and evil. They asserted their will against God's will.

Peck's reading of the passage in Genesis 3 is totally different from this interpretation. Their sin, according to Peck, is that they did not question God regarding the prohibition He had given them. They should have asked Him why they could not eat of the tree, since it didn't make much sense to them.

> Instead they went ahead and broke God's law without ever understanding the reason behind the law, without taking the effort to challenge God directly, question his authority or even communicate with Him on a reasonably adult level. They listened to the serpent, but they failed to get God's side of the story before they acted. . . . It is this missing step that is the essence of sin. The step missing is the step of de-

bate. Adam and Eve could have set up a debate between the serpent and God, but in failing to do so they failed to obtain God's side of the question.[7]

Peck then seeks to apply this original statement of sin to the current state of human decision making:

> Our failure to conduct—or to conduct fully and whole heartedly—this internal debate between good and evil is the cause of those evil actions that constitute sin. In debating the wisdom of a proposed course of action, human beings routinely fail to obtain God's side of the issue. They fail to consult or listen to the god within them, the knowledge of rightness which inherently resides with the minds of all mankind. We make this failure because we are lazy. It is work to hold these internal debates. These internal debates require time and energy just to conduct them. . . .[8]

Theories on Origin of Evil

According to Peck, only three major theological explanations for evil currently exist. First, there is the idea of a non-dualism (actually a pseudo-dualism since these religions are pantheistic) espoused by Hinduism and Buddhism. Under this paradigm, evil is envisioned as the equal opposite of good. For example, life has an antonym we call death, peace is opposed by war, the opposite of love is hate. In the same way, explains Peck, the first model views evil as merely the antithesis of good.

Peck then suggests that there is a second way to understand evil. This second model holds that evil is distinct from good, but evil nonetheless is a part of God's creation. This is a finite dualism. Peck explains that in order for

God to grant His creation free will and individual volition, we, as creatures made in God's image, must be allowed to make wrong, even evil, choices. Peck labels this second possible explanation for evil "integrated dualism."

The third and final model for sin is "diabolic dualism." To Peck this third option is the system employed by traditional Christianity. Under this view, "evil is regarded as being not of God's creation but a ghastly cancer beyond His control."[9] And according to Peck, this is the only one of the three viewpoints that deals adequately with the issue of murder and the murderer.

The true view is in reality a view not offered by Peck. We shall look at it in more detail below, but in brief it is that evil came into existence apart from God's creation, that He allows His moral creatures—angels and humans—to make a moral choice—free will—but that He will bring an end to sin through the death of Christ and that the end of sin will occur in history.

Peck would probably agree that the problem of evil is an old issue expounded on by both great and small thinkers from time immemorial.[10] Though there are probably a dozen different ways to explain the existence or nonexistence of evil, for expediency's sake it is understandable that Peck groups all theories into three basic categories. It is unfortunate, however, that he did not spend more time researching this issue, especially the view of evil espoused by the Bible. What Peck considers to be the traditional Christian model is far from orthodox, and I suggest he would be hard pressed to demonstrate that any of the apostles taught "diabolic dualism."

One could arguably state that Peck has made an accurate evaluation concerning his first model of evil. There does in fact exist a strong emphasis among many Eastern religions, Taoism in particular, on placing our existence and all reality within a dual framework. One must realize, however, that this is not so much a model for explaining how evil came about or why it exists, but rather a simple acknowledgment or proof that it exists.

The second model concerning evil, which Peck quickly passes over, is better known as the Free Will theory. Unfortunately, Peck makes an unforgivable modification to this theory and then gives his new creation the ambiguous title of "integrated dualism." When Peck proposes that "evil is distinct from good but is nonetheless of God's creation,"[11] he is in fact suggesting that God created evil. Neither the Bible nor the Free Will theory ever suggest that God established evil as a part of His creation. Genesis 1:31 states concerning the creation, "God saw all that he had made, and it was very good." God is not the Father of sin; rather the Bible tells us that it was by Adam that sin entered the world (Romans 5:12). Though the God of the Bible may allow us to sin, it is important to note that the Christian God despises evil (Psalm 5:4).

An Alternate Model for the Origin of Evil

In all actuality, if there is any one traditional Christian model concerning evil, the Free Will viewpoint would probably hold the strongest claim to the title. Peck's presentation of this view is unfortunately a distortion of the perspective. Proponents of the accurate portrayal of free will explain that God granted Adam the ability to decide between obedience and rebellion. One of the strongest advocates of this viewpoint was Thomas Aquinas. Aquinas was very successful in promoting the idea that God allows people to commit evil deeds, but not because God is unable to stop evil or unconcerned about His creation. Rather, Aquinas argues for a loving, omnipotent God who grants humanity the ability to make choices, whatever they may be.

Peck suggests that his third model is the viewpoint employed by traditional Christianity. As he offers no external or historical support for this statement one wonders how he comes to this conclusion. In fact, Scripture opposes this third theory of God and evil. When Peck says that evil is a cancer beyond God's control, Peck is essentially proposing that God may be good but He is powerless to eradicate evil. *As to who this god is that Peck is talking about, one thing is definite; he is not the God of the Bible.* As a Christian, Peck should know that nothing is beyond the power of the true God. The Bible states unequivocally that God is omnipotent (Genesis 18:14; Jeremiah 32:27; Matthew 19:26).

Essentially Peck's second and third models can be considered modifications of two heretical explanations for why God allows evil in our world. Peck's second model basically suggests that evil exists because God created it and frankly God is not concerned that it is here on our planet. This God is powerful but He is also unconcerned and withdrawn.

The third model which Peck devises is just the opposite. Under this theory, God is opposed to evil; in fact, He probably hates it, but unfortunately He is not strong enough to remove it from human existence. So this God is good and compassionate, but He is not powerful enough to put an end to sin.

As we have already seen, none of these theories qualifies as Christian because the Word of God reveals that God is not only inherently loving, opposed to evil, but He is also the omnipotent and sovereign deity who can accomplish all things. The Scriptures proclaim that evil exists in the world; in fact, Christ Jesus died on the cross for the very reason of removing the sins of mankind (1 John 1:7).

Peck at least admits that people do in fact commit evil (though his definition is not a completely biblical view); this truly is a rarity among most therapists today. In this age of relativism and anti-morality, especially within the social sciences, it is refreshing to find someone who acknowledges the fact that people willfully commit evil acts. Peck admits that evil exists, but considers evil to be a "mystery."[12] In many ways evil is mysterious; as sinful beings we cannot always detect nor understand the various evils that exist in and around us.

Human experience is far too limited to be able to fully examine and assess evil. Fortunately God has given us some insights concerning sin and evil. Unfortunately Peck has either neglected to read the Bible's views on this issue or he simply misunderstands what Scripture has to say. Furthermore, Peck continues to claim that he represents the Christian perspective, even though his representative statements in no way correspond to orthodox Christian theology.

Contrary to what Peck may believe, traditional Christianity does not support the idea that "the universe is locked in a titanic struggle between the forces of good and evil, between God and the devil."[13] To make this statement would be to put God and Satan on an equal level, and this is surely not the case. God has already prepared a place of eternal punishment for the devil (Matthew 25:41). Furthermore, the Bible declares that the devil is destined for eternal suffering and torment (Revelation 20:10). Put simply, the devil and his evil followers are doomed to suffer eternal punishment, and they have no hope of salvation, for even they know the time is coming when they will be judged by God (see Matthew 8:28-29).

Another aspect of Dr. Peck's understanding of a "traditional Christian model"[14] that questions whether the individual soul will be won to God or to the devil is concerned with whether or not we have the correct question. The correct question is not whether the individual soul will finally decide *between* God and the devil, but whether the individual soul will decide *for* God, for the soul is already completely, irretrievably and wholly within the sphere of the devil's influence. It is completely without recourse or redemption within its own right.

By failing to recognize this point as one of primary importance, we cannot recognize the "sin nature" within a child. "Everything that does not come from faith is sin" (Romans 14:23) is the measure of sin. Furthermore, "[i]f we claim to be without sin, we deceive ourselves" (1 John

1:8). Once we accept this simple truth, then we can start to see the sin within us, even to the point of recognizing the sin nature in a child. Any parent who has raised children has but to recall his or her child's temper when he or she has been denied something that the parent deemed to be improper. Only through the grace of God do some "leave" the camp of the devil. This will be seen more clearly as we consider the different aspects of our sin nature, our helplessness before it and the final gift of God that provided a means for a person to be redeemed from his or her own nature.

Realizing the dangers of evil, Peck believes evil should be viewed in a proper perspective. He suggests:

> The only valid reason to recognize human evil is to heal it wherever we can, and (as is currently most often the case) when we cannot, to study it further that we might discover how to heal it in specific instances and eventually wipe its ugliness off the face of the earth.[15]

Does this mean that Peck believes that given enough time and study, evil (also read sin) will be eradicated from human existence? The Bible describes evil as something inherent within human nature (Romans 1:18-21). By nature man is evil, and because we transgress God's holy laws we are convicted by our sin and sentenced to die. Peck, however, must not believe the Bible when it says, "For the wages of sin is death" (Romans 6:23). In fact, we know that Peck does not believe this statement because he writes, "Evil has nothing to do with natural death. . . ."[16] And although Peck believes that evil does not bring death to the body, he is more than willing to concede that evil may be passed from person to person via biological inheritance.[17]

Peck does not argue that all evil originates within the genetic makeup, however. Rather, Peck assumes that since almost all diseases have physical roots, evil probably also has some connection to our DNA. In order to explain how evil manifests itself, Peck has chosen to accept a classical model of evil championed by many philosophers for the last several hundred years. Under this model, evil can be understood as coming from one of two sources. The first type of evil is known as natural evil; this branch encompasses such things as death and destruction caused by fire, flood, earthquakes and famines. All types of evil which do not originate from the individual but from the natural world can be classified as natural evil. The other brand of evil that Peck describes is known as moral evil, though Peck prefers to call it human evil. Under this category reside all the various types of evil stemming from human action, such as murder, robbery and child abuse.[18]

To Peck, the real question is not why is there evil in the world, but rather why is there any good in the world. Peck states that "... it probably makes more sense to assume this is a naturally evil world that has somehow been mysteriously 'contaminated' by goodness, rather than the other way around."[19] The riddle, then, is why do humans commit good deeds when evil surrounds them on all sides? The answer to this question, and to the many others that Peck raises concerning evil, can be found within the pages of Scripture. If Peck would only search the Bible, he would discover that what he presents as a Christian perspective is something else entirely.

For instance, not only does Peck see the biblical Satan as a neuter "it," but he also has a hard time believing that Satan even exists. Though he claims to be a Christian dedicated to Scripture, he is willing to teach his patients that they not only have the power to spring Satan into existence, but they can also, through their own diligence, "end his existence."[20] Here Peck proves his earlier statements that evil is a dangerous area to be studying, for he gives poor advice. Readers may find it interesting to note that Michael the Archangel himself, when arguing with Satan over the body of Moses, did not even dare to bring a slanderous accusation against the devil (Jude 1:9). Not only is Satan a real being (see Job 1:6; Luke 22:3; Revelation 20:7), he is also a very powerful angel we should not even dream of defeating on our own.[21]

Additionally Peck holds a certain optimism concerning evil that, though hopeful, is entirely devoid of biblical revelation. Contrary to what Peck may believe, the human race will never wipe out the ugliness of evil from this earth. Obviously if evil is partly genetic, as Peck assumes, then it seems it would be impossible to eradicate evil by doing anything less than genetically altering every person on this planet, a highly unlikely procedure. If, on the other hand, evil is socially created and disseminated, then it would mean evil would have to be extracted from our culture and totally withdrawn from society. One wonders what kind of strong-arm tactics would have to be made in order to keep people in line—and wouldn't these severe limitations on self-autonomy touch on being evil themselves? And finally, even if by some miracle we are able to remove all human evil from the world, what can we possibly do to stop natural evil from operating on its normal course?

A Biblical Perspective on Sin

Dr. Peck in general defines sin as our failure to conduct, fully and wholeheartedly, an internal debate within ourselves between good actions and evil actions. He then states this failure is "the cause of those evil actions that constitute sin."[22] However, this position is far from the biblical representation of sin.

Biblically speaking, sin is far more than a choice between actions, whether good or evil; it is a willful decision to exercise my will above the will of God. Sin is also a spiritual component of humanity that is both deeply and irretrievably entwined within the personality, within the psyche of humanity itself. It is an absolute part of humanity, an integral component of a person that is "in him" or "in her" and "dwells" with him or her (see Romans 8:20, 23).

This can be seen as we consider the power of sin. Sin has a power over people that surpasses their choices or ability to debate an action. For example, the Apostle Paul regards sin as a power that not only dwells within a person, but it also reigns over the person; the person is a slave to it (see Romans 5:12; 6:6, 14). This is what Dr. Peck fails to recognize, and as a result he fails to grasp that this is precisely and ultimately where the problem lies, shrouded within a penumbra of personal rationalization and self-denial.

So pervasive is the sin within a person that it can appear to be almost invisible. For example, the Bible states that pride is a sin (see Mark 7:22, 1 John 2:16, et al.). In fact, many people recognize that pride is a sin. However, few, if any of us, understand the depth of the sin of pride. One classic biblical example of the sin of pride is that of Nebuchadnezzar, the king of Babylon, as he admired the great city that he had helped to build, including the famous Hanging Gardens of Babylon. Nebuchadnezzar believed that he had the right as the king of Babylon to take for himself the majesty and glory of the construction of the city. Daniel records the statement of Nebuchadnezzar: "Is not this the great Babylon I have built as the royal residence, by my mighty power and for the glory of my majesty?" (Daniel 4:30).

The problem inherent with Nebuchadnezzar was that he believed that he was the ultimate creator of all that he saw. He believed that without his express purpose and will, none of the work would have been accomplished. He alone was responsible for the grandeur of Babylon. Fortunately for him the Lord saw fit to correct his misunderstanding, to reveal the error that his pride had brought about. Daniel records the judgment that fell upon him for this overt sin: "[Nebuchadnezzar] will be driven away from people and will live with the wild animals" (Daniel 4:32). Perhaps most instructive of all within this section of Scripture is the final response of Nebuchadnezzar at the end of his period of banishment. He raised his eyes toward heaven, and his reason returned to him. Immediately he blessed the Most High and praised and honored Him (Daniel 4:34), for he finally understood what the sin of pride was.

This sin of pride is not necessarily contained within the overt statement, "Is not this the great Babylon I have built as the royal residence, by my mighty power and for the glory of my majesty?" made by Nebuchadnezzar. Rather it is contained within the man himself in his desire to establish for himself the claim. We see the egocentricity of Nebuchadnezzar that eliminates the assistance of untold numbers of other people who actually did the work. It is a statement against God; it is a form of revolt against God, for it is God alone who is the Creator of all things. It is a statement that says, "The glory is mine alone for the accomplishment, even if you, God, created everything—including me—that I used to create my own work."

This depth and bondage to sin, this "hidden" perspective to the nature of sin is that which requires a solution apart from humankind, a solution that has nothing to do with the intellect or experience of an individual. This solution has been provided to us through the grace of God in the form of the sacrificial gift of the life and ultimately the death of Jesus, a death that was consummated on the cross of Calvary. The failure to understand this hidden perspective of the nature of sin is the primary reason why people fail to see the need for redemption. The apostle Paul put the need to understand the crucifixion very succinctly when he said, "For what I received I passed on to you as of first importance: that Christ died for our sins according to the Scriptures, that he was buried, that he was raised on the third day according to the Scriptures, and that he appeared to Peter, and then to the Twelve" (1 Corinthians 15:3-5).

Dr. Peck's inability to grasp the complete nature of the crucifixion as an atoning sacrifice, one that allows Christians to confess sin and be forgiven, cleansed "from all unrighteousness" (1 John 1:9) allows him to easily slip into the error of simply seeing a psychological solution to what is actually a spiritual problem. He equates a "natural" psychological relationship to be the same as a spiritual (or ontological) relationship. However, the differences are as great as night versus day. Through his understanding of evil as a form of mental "laziness," he presumes that sin is only part of the natural psychological phenomena of the human species, not part of the nature of humans, but rather part of their conscious/subconscious self-deterministic approach to life. As such, says Peck, it is treatable as a disease or mental disorder. Yet we have already seen that the sin nature is an integral part of human nature: "In the radical depravity of man there is necessarily hidden his true nature," says Karl Barth, "in his total degeneracy, his original form."[23]

A more correct approach to the relationship of sin with natural psychology has been provided by Ernest Becker. He explains:

> [S]in and neurosis are two ways of talking about the same thing. Neurosis is the result of our denying the reality or mortality of our creatureliness. Faced with the agonizing terror of being a self in light of the knowledge of ourselves as both a mortal body and an unlimited spirit, the existing self turns away from this task of becoming a person and reaches out for security in some manageable exercise with clearly defined limits. Faith, as the full expression of personal reality, means that one would be able to live before the divine Spirit in absolute freedom from this paralyzing conflict between the spirit and the flesh. One narrows down one's existence by identifying the self with what is within our grasp and control. In seeking to control our own existence and escape the terror of life, we become obsessed with what appears to give that

sense of security and continuity. This is not only neurotic behavior, but it is also a failure to become a person by risking oneself to the transcendent—to the idea of God. Therefore, sin and neurosis alike are symptoms of an underlying defection at the level of our true being.[24]

Dr. Peck Fails to Separate Guilt from Sin

Dr. Peck has failed to see that humanity is guilty and deserves whatever punishment a wholly righteous God would require.

The Bible is the Word of God. It is His law for people because it teaches them what sin actually is—lawlessness (1 John 3:4). It is rebelling against God and falling short of the glory of God (Romans 3:23). The law does not save them from sin (Acts 13:39, 1 Timothy 1:9-10). On the contrary, the biblical law requires restitution before God. "When a man or woman wrongs another in any way and so is unfaithful to the LORD, that person is guilty and must confess the sin he has committed. He must make full restitution for his wrong, add one fifth to it and give it all to the person he has wronged" (Numbers 5:6-7).

Dr. Peck appears to acknowledge the existence of this guilt even though he does not recognize its source. For example, he states, "Examination of the world without is never as personally painful as examination of the world within, and it is certainly because of the pain involved in a life of genuine self-examination that the majority steer away from it."[25] In his estimation this process of inner examination is most "unnatural and hence more human," and thus more rewarding. Yet I submit that the reason for the apparent contradiction between being "unnaturally introspective" for the purpose of growth and the essence of psychotherapeutic growth is nothing more than what God has been trying to tell us for thousands of years. "[Y]ou desire truth in the inner parts; you teach me wisdom in the inmost place" (Psalm 51:6) and "the truth will set you free" (John 8:32). King David learned this valuable lesson some three thousand years ago after he had been confronted by Nathan the prophet concerning his adulterous relationship with Bathsheba and the subsequent murder of her husband, Uriah. He recorded it for us in Psalm 51:1-4:

> Have mercy on me, O God,
>   according to your unfailing love;
> according to your great compassion
>   blot out my transgressions.
> Wash away all my iniquity
>   and cleanse me from my sin.
>
> For I know my transgressions,
>   and my sin is always before me.
> Against you, you only, have I sinned
>   and done what is evil in your sight,
> so that you are proved right when you speak
>   and justified when you judge.

Clearly David not only recognized his guilt, but he also recognized that his primary responsibility for that guilt was directly to God. He was not concerned with "balancing" his life between conflicting sets of relationships as a juggler performs his circus act. Rather he was concerned with acknowledging his guilt and submitting himself before the Lord completely so the Lord could balance his life. This is not an avoidance of truth or responsibility; rather it is the acknowledgement of ultimate truth and responsibility before God. This acknowledgement is critical, for we know that the personal commission of sin in whatever form brings guilt and condemnation, which require death. "For the wages of sin is death, but the gift of God is eternal life in Christ Jesus our Lord" (Romans 6:23).

Dr. Peck Fails to See Condemnation

Dr. Peck has failed to acknowledge that the foundational position of humanity is one of condemnation. He can find no explanation as to why the Christian God of light (1 John 1:5) and love (1 John 4:16), in whom there is no darkness (read that "sin") should condemn. On the other hand, we have already seen that people are by nature full of sin, and subject only to wrath.[26] This is not simply an isolated doctrine or an empty philosophy. Many people have recognized this position and so recorded their own understanding of it.

For example, when they "saw that the fruit of the tree was good for food and pleasing to the eye, and also desirable for gaining wisdom" and Adam and Eve, contrary to God's proscription, decided to eat the forbidden fruit, they recognized their error. This knowledge of sin was confirmed when God delivered His judgment upon them: "Cursed is the ground because of you" (Genesis 3:17). This disobedience to God's command brought condemnation.

Another example can be seen when the psalmist writes:

> Do you rulers indeed speak justly?
> Do you judge uprightly among men?
> No, in your heart you devise injustice,
>   and your hands mete out violence on the
>   earth.
> Even from birth the wicked go astray;
>   from the womb they are wayward and speak
>   lies. (Psalm 58:1-3)

Notice how this waywardness is from birth. Babies, for all of their sweetness and joy, do have a sin nature.

One aspect of estrangement is that we often determine to no longer acknowledge God's existence.[27] This attitude is frequently seen when an individual either witnesses or is the recipient of some significant act of evil. Anyone who experienced the horrors of war would be tempted to conclude that there was no God. The Russian author Dostoevsky in his novel *The Brothers Karamazov* has a classic example in the story of a boy who injures a general's dog. In retaliation, the general sets a pack of dogs on the boy to tear him to pieces in front of his mother's eyes. After Ivan Karamazov narrates this story to his brother, Alyosha, he explains how he cannot accept that such a world is God's world: "It's not God that I don't accept, Alyosha, only I most respectfully return him the ticket."[28] This estrangement from God can and does produce such results in many millions of people with tremendous regularity. Yet we must note that it is Ivan Karamazov who is "returning the ticket" to God, it is man who maintains the state of separation.

This is the problem. Humanity is condemned. In professing to be wise, we have become foolish (Romans 1:22). Therefore God has given us over to the lusts of our own hearts, that we through our own devices might become filled with unrighteousness, wickedness, greed, evil, envy, murder, strife, deceit and malice (Romans 1:29-30).

Once we grasp this unwelcome truth, that we stand condemned before God, then and only then are we ready to seek after God's remedy.

Dr. Peck Fails to See the Redemptive Message

Since Dr. Peck doesn't understand the condemnation that humanity is under, he doesn't see the need for redemption and the fact that redemption has been provided for us by God. The Bible describes both the need for this redemption of humanity and the method in which redemption has been provided for us. This redemption centers around the person of Jesus Christ, the Son of God. Specifically it centers on His sinless life, His sacrificial death by crucifixion and the ultimate proof of the resurrection.

Biblical redemption is the act of purchasing one individual through the sacrifice of another. It does not necessarily

195

require a one-to-one relationship, i.e., one person for only one other person. Rather, biblically speaking, redemption has occurred through the sacrifice of one individual for many other individuals—for example, the sacrifice of Jesus for all of humankind. Redemption is seen as a gift of God to His people (Romans 3:24; Psalm 111:9, 130:7). It is through the life of His Son Jesus (Matthew 3:17; Romans 3:24; 1 Corinthians 1:30) coming as a sacrifice for humanity. He is a "ransom for many" (Matthew 20:28; Mark 10:45), a purchase (1 Corinthians 6:20) through the gift of His blood, the ultimate sacrifice through the surrender of His own life (Acts 20:28).

For our purposes, Alister McGrath presents the cross in a very clear light in his book, *The Mystery of the Cross*. He explains:

> [T]he cross is a key by which the ambiguities of human existence may be unlocked, casting light on the situation in which the Christian now finds himself in the world. Knowing that the one who was crucified was raised, and knowing that he himself has been crucified with Christ, the believer may make the crucified Christ the guiding principle of his life.[29]

This understanding has a tremendous power in setting the believer free from the anxieties of the world because the cross helps him or her to see that anxiety is unwarranted in the light of the resurrection. The apostle Paul explained this concept: "May I never boast except in the cross of our Lord Jesus Christ" (Galatians 6:14).

In conclusion then, there is a problem with evil. It is not something that constitutes a hidden dark side in humans. Dr. Peck tells the story of "George"[30] in which George was "good" up until the day in which he made a pact with the devil, which caused him to start to become "evil." But evil does not usually have a psychological boundary whereby a person simply goes from good to evil by one simple choice. Evil is but one form or one outward manifestation of sin. It derives its existence from the effects of sin upon a person. *Sin is real.* Sin is a spiritual, ontological part of humanity. Sin has been with people, every person, ever since our forebears, Adam and Eve, ate the fruit within the garden of Eden. Sin is present in us from within the womb until the grave. Sin cannot be eradicated from a person's life until the person acknowledges his or her sinful nature before God and prayerfully asks God to help him or her to overcome his or her own sinful nature. Only through the help of God will there be success. Only in this process will whatever evil present within a person have any hope of being eradicated.

Endnotes

1. Peck, M. Scott. *People of the Lie* (New York: Simon and Schuster, 1983), p. 209.

2. Peck, M. Scott. *Further Along the Road Less Traveled* (New York: Simon and Schuster, 1993), p. 157.

3. Peck, *People*, p. 10.

4. Peck, M. Scott. *The Road Less Traveled* (New York: Simon & Schuster, 1978), p. 133.

5. Peck, *The Road*, p. 271.

6. Peck, *The Road*, pp. 271-272.

7. Peck, *The Road*, pp. 272-273.

8. Peck, *The Road*, p. 273.

9. Peck, *People*, p. 46.

10. Augustine, Aquinas, Hick and Barth, to name just a few, are well known for their writings in the field of theodicy (the problem of God and evil).

11. Peck, *People*, p. 46.

12. Peck, *People*, pp. 41, 39.

13. Peck, *People*, p. 37.

14. Peck, *People*, p. 37.

15. Peck, *People*, p. 44.

16. Peck, *People*, p. 44.

17. Peck, *People,* p. 45.

18. Peck, *People,* p. 45.

19. Peck, *People,* p. 41.

20. Peck, *People,* p. 33.

21. Peck has a discussion on exorcism (*People of the Lie,* pp. 182-211) that I have chosen not to interact with in the main body of the book due to space limitations. The major difficulty with Peck's views is that the exorcisms do not seem to equate with those given in the New Testament and may be done equally by non-Christians as by Christians.

22. Peck, *The Road,* pp. 272-273.

23. Barth, Karl, quoted in Ray S. Anderson, *On Being Human: Essays in Theological Anthropology* (Grand Rapids: William B. Eerdman's Publishing Company), p. 30.

24. Becker, Ernest. The Denial of Death (New York: MacMillan, 1973), p. 196, quoted in Anderson, p. 94.

25. Peck, *The Road,* p. 52.

26. Romans 1:18-23 has a graphically clear statement of the position of man before God.

27. Many people claim that they do not know God, that they have never known God and that He doesn't exist. Unfortunately the biblical picture is that all people do know God because "what may be known about God is plain to them, because God has made it plain to them" (Romans 1:19).

28. Quoted from Alister E. McGrath, *The Mystery of the Cross* (Grand Rapids: Zondervan Publishing House, 1988), p. 117.

29. McGrath, p. 33.

30. Peck, *People,* pp. 15-35.

CHAPTER 9

Taking a Wrong Turn:
Dr. Peck's Basic Theology

*I'm one of those people who tend to do their writing
first and their research afterwards.*

—M. Scott Peck[1]

*Christian doctrine, on the whole, approaches reality
more closely than do the other great religions, although I also believe that on occasion the others may
come a bit closer.*

—M. Scott Peck[2]

*. . . [C]ontend for the faith which was once for all
entrusted to the saints.*

—Jude 3

Since M. Scott Peck has vowed that he has embraced
Christianity, one would expect him to depart from the
anti-Christian views he espoused in his first book, *The
Road Less Traveled*. In that book, as I have demonstrated in
chapters 6 and 7, Dr. Peck uses much Christian terminology and even adopts aspects of Christian thought, yet he
deviates significantly from the essential teachings of the

historic Christian faith. In the subjects discussed in this chapter, this is no less true.

Peck rejects the integrity of both the Old and New Testaments, views God as a sincere but impotent deity, an evolving God rather than the unchanging One, and as being both male and female.

Jesus, in Peck's theology, is not the God presented in the creeds of the church. In the historic confessions of the church Jesus shares the same attributes as the Father and the Spirit; He is fully God. To Peck Jesus is also an androgynous being, one who has both male and female sexuality. Moreover, in Peck's perspective, He is not really our Savior from sin. His death is an example for us rather than an atonement for our sin.

He still maintains that salvation is not a meritless act of God done on our behalf, but instead is our reaching toward perfection through the process of evolution.

Finally, Peck combines aspects of Protestant and Roman Catholic theology on heaven and purgatory that he likes. He rejects the doctrine of a place of punishment after death.

Peck's View of Scripture

I dealt with Peck's view of Scripture in chapter 6, developing his perspective of relative truth in contrast to the absolute truth presented in the Bible. Here we will look more at Peck's view of Scripture, how Peck interprets the Bible and his criticism of those who hold to a high view of Scripture.

The Bible Is an Errant Book

To Peck, not only is the story of Adam and Eve simply myth and the Gospels an inaccurate history, but this indictment stands true for the entire Bible. Peck declares:

> [The Bible] is a mixture of legend, some of which is true and some of which is not true. It

is a mixture of very accurate history and not so accurate history. It is a mixture of outdated rules and some pretty good rules. It is a mixture of myth and metaphor.[3]

For Peck, those who take the Bible as the inerrant Word of God detract from the Bible[4] and "strangely misuse" it.[5] He seems to believe that the only options open to us are to accept a rigid literalism or to accept it as errant and often mythical.[6]

In passing his sweeping judgment on the Bible, Dr. Peck is attacking the very foundation of the Christian faith. In advocating a fallible Bible, he is denying its inspiration by God, unless he wishes to say that God is fallible. Given his view of God, this may not be a problem for him. Nonetheless, Peck reveals his ignorance of the historical accuracy of the Scriptures. Both Israel and the early church considered the Bible to be a true record of real historical events.[7] This approach is considerably different from the writings of other world religions. The Hebrew and Christian Scriptures, however, are not merely presenting a good way of life. They are seeking to describe a true interaction between the Creator of the universe and human beings created by Him. If the events described did not occur, then the view of reality, the faith believed, leaves the faithful as fools in a fake religion, dedicating their lives for an eternity with a God that will never exist (see for example 1 Corinthians 15:1-19).

Scripture purports to be revelation from the God of the universe who has entered into space and time to communicate with real historical persons (Luke 1:23-38) and save and dwell with His people (Genesis 3, 12; Exodus 3; John 1:14). This is the plain, non-forced reading of the text.

Jesus declared that the Scriptures cannot err (John 10:35); Paul says that Scripture is God-breathed; Peter testifies that he was among those who heard God's voice from heaven, "the word of the prophets made more certain" (2

Peter 1:19-21). Though specious arguments have been made against the veracity of the Bible and endless attempts have been made to demonstrate historical or moral error, all attempts have been unsuccessful.[8] Throughout the last several centuries many important historical and archaeological findings have demonstrated the veracity of the biblical data. None has shown the Bible to be in error.

Twisting the Text: Peck's Method of Biblical Interpretation

Many people may view Dr. Peck as a lay theologian, but Dr. Peck betrays a serious lack of knowledge about biblical interpretation. He seemingly does not understand that persons who believe in literal interpretation generally mean by that phrase that the Bible is to be taken in the plain sense of the text unless language is obviously figurative.

"How are we to interpret the Bible?" Peck asks. "Indeed the Bible is a collection of paradoxical stories. . . . It is a mixture of legend, some of which is true and some of which is not true. . . . It is a mixture of very accurate history and not so accurate history. . . . It is a mixture of myth and metaphor."[9]

If the Bible does actually contain untrue legends, inaccurate history and myth, then Peck offers no evidence to support his statements. Yet when an open-minded and honest evaluation of the historical records, both secular and sacred, (not to mention the archaeological records) is undertaken, we find the Bible vindicated. Yet Peck claims:

> [T]he term "fundamentalist" is a misnomer. The more proper term is "inerrantists," those who believe that the Bible is not only the divinely inspired word of God, but the actual transcribed, unaltered word of God, and that it is subject to only one kind of literal interpretation, namely theirs. Such thinking, to my mind, only impoverishes the Bible.[10]

Dr. Peck may be sincere in his desire to present the teachings of Scripture, but unfortunately he is sincerely wrong in practically every place he speaks about biblical passages; the illustrations serve to demonstrate this likelihood.

Do We "Pluck Out Our Eyes" and Lose Sight of the Meaning?

Peck's statement above is simply not true and has cast an inaccurate and blatant disregard for those claiming the inerrancy of the Bible. Peck attempts to bolster his argument with an emotional example, speaking of a young man who had gouged out one of his eyes because Jesus said, "[I]f your eye causes you to sin, pluck it out" (Mark 9:47). Perhaps Peck should open his eyes to the truth that the Bible does teach, rather than coming to it with a presuppositional "one-eyed" view. If we were to take the Bible as only non-figurative truth, then Jesus was a vine (John 15:1), a loaf of bread (John 6:35), a cup of wine (Mark 14:23-24), a mother hen (Matthew 23:37).

Peck has built straw men and seems happy when he is able to knock them down. In the midst of the plain, obvious meaning of a text, there are figurative expressions that most of us understand.[11]

Another problem with Dr. Peck's interpretation of the text of Scripture is that he presumes certain understanding of words that are really foreign to meanings found in standard scholarly sources. Neither does he read the various texts he deals with in context.

Poor in Spirit or Understanding?

Dr. Peck encourages the "fully mature person" to be a "truth seeker." But is Peck willing to stand up to a truthful, historical and evidential appraisal of his incredibly incorrect hermeneutics and therefore his utter misconception of who and what the Jesus of the Bible was and is? If he will, then he may actually find the correct road that leads to life.

If not, he will continue to do great damage to the Scripture as evidenced in his treatment of the "poor in spirit" in the Sermon on the Mount. On this text Peck states:

> You know, when Jesus gave His big sermon, the first words out of His mouth were: "Blessed are the poor in spirit." There are a number of ways to translate "poor in spirit," but on an intellectual level, the best translation is "confused." Blessed are the confused. If you ask why Jesus might have said that, then I must point out to you that confusion leads to a search for clarification and with that search comes a great deal of learning.[12]

It is obvious here that it is Dr. Peck who is the one thoroughly confused, in the true sense of the word. For no such rendering is allowed by the Greek language in which the Gospel according to Matthew was originally written. When one takes this "big sermon" in its context, along with the whole of the New Testament, it is abundantly clear that what Jesus meant was that we as humans are incapable of reaching a level of righteousness by our own works or deeds. The one who is poor in spirit recognizes that his or her condition before God is lacking and recognizes this spiritual poverty, calling out for grace to live for God. Paul wrote in his letter to the Romans: "[F]or all have sinned and fall short of the glory of God" (Romans 3:23). When one comes to this realization, we are "poor in spirit," capable then of receiving the other benefits of the kingdom of God.

Give Up Your Children?

Dr. Peck states that one of the "great blessings" of his life was an almost total absence of religious education.[13] Yet when we list yet another example of how incorrect his understanding of the Bible and its truths and teachings are, we would rightly conclude that he still possesses an absence of religious knowledge.

Peck offers an incredibly wrong interpretation of the Genesis 22 account of Abraham obeying God's command to sacrifice his only son, Isaac. Peck discounts the episode as being another myth, but again offers no evidence or support for such a claim. He continues:

> Interpreted metaphorically, this wonderful story—or myth—teaches us that the time comes when we have to give up our children. Yes, they were gifts to us and given to our keeping—but not forever. Holding on to them beyond a certain point can be extremely destructive to them, and ourselves as well.[14]

Does one need a doctorate in theology in order to understand the simple truths and lessons of the Bible? No. But one may need to be tainted with worldly psychobabble in order to come up with such a misunderstanding of a simple story. First of all there are at least two aspects that encompass this account.

The first aspect is the lesson taught to all who will hear of humanity's obedience to the will of God. God knew that if anything stood between Him and Abraham's worship of Him, it was his rightful son, Isaac. So God tested Abraham and called him to do something very difficult—to sacrifice his only son (that is the son through whom he would fulfill his agreement with God). When God saw Abraham's obedient faith, He stopped Abraham at the last instant.

The second aspect is seen in Abraham's statement in 22:4, that both he *and* Isaac would return. Could this be Abraham's belief that God would resurrect Isaac after he had been sacrificed? Yes, as the writer of Hebrews reveals, "Abraham reasoned that God could raise the dead, and figuratively speaking, he did receive Isaac back from death" (11:19). The typology here is clear: Isaac is a type of Christ in both His sacrificial role to redeem the world and as our resurrected Lord and Savior!

Peck Blames the Church

Peck believes that theologians and the church have been responsible for much of the lack of community experienced by people today.[15] At another time, however, he says it is the failure to practice its theology that is the church's problem. He quotes G.K. Chesterson on this: "Christianity hasn't been tried and found wanting, it has been found difficult and untried."[16]

I say a hearty "Amen!" to the quote from Chesterson, but this does not excuse anyone from being an active participant in Christianity; it is a call to a more faithful Christian faith. Since Peck rejects practically every aspect of Christian theology and morality, he is certainly not the one to call the church to account.

In reality, Dr. Peck believes that the theologians of the church are not the ones to properly direct the church in its theology. One does not have to read his books very long to discover that he instead puts much confidence in the assured results of psychiatry and considers science as "holy" and "godly."[17] In the mind of Dr. Peck, the church is dogmatic and science is seeking for truth; theology is nebulous, but science seeks to understand the real world.

Even though he believes he has better ways to gain proper knowledge than those provided by orthodox Christian thinkers, Peck does tell us that he does not view one religion as just as good as another. Apparently Christianity is the best understanding of God, although other religions also provide helpful information:

> On the intellectual level, the reason I became a Christian is that I gradually came to believe that, on the whole, Christian doctrine approaches the reality of God and reality in general more closely than the other great religions. This doesn't mean that there isn't a great deal to be learned from the other religions. There's

an enormous amount to be learned, and it is the responsibility of any educated Christian to garner as much of the wisdom of other religious traditions as she or he possibly can.

Perhaps the greatest sin of the Christian church has been that particular brand of arrogance, or narcissism, that impels so many Christians to feel they have got God all sewn up and put in their back pocket. Those who think that they've got the whole truth and nothing but the truth, and that those other poor slobs who believe differently are necessarily not saved, as far as I'm concerned have a very small God. They don't realize the truth that God is bigger than their own theology. As I've said, God is not ours to possess, but we are His or Hers to be possessed by. And there is nothing that does more than this narrow-minded narcissism to de-evangelize Christianity.[18]

Hardly has any other statement made by Peck revealed his total misunderstanding about the essence of Christian truth more than the quote given above. Surely there are correct aspects about God present in other religions. This was true of the religions of the nations around Israel in Old Testament times. It was true of the Greek and Roman worlds of New Testament times (Acts 17). *But most of what they taught about God directly contradicted what God revealed about Himself in the Old and New Testament communities*. God didn't say, "Go to the nations and learn of Me." Jesus said, "Therefore go and make disciples of all nations, baptizing them in the name of the Father and of the Son and of the Holy Spirit, and teaching them to obey everything I have commanded you" (Matthew 28:19-20). Peck would consider such an approach narrow and dogmatic.

It is not arrogant to accept God for who He has revealed Himself to be; it *is* arrogant for Dr. Peck to reject the revelation that God has given and substitute his insights from Zen Buddhism. Certainly there is more to God than He has revealed, but we are held accountable to embrace what He has revealed. Orthodox Christianity does have the truth about God. Rather than de-evangelizing Christianity, as Peck says, this truth about the reality of God is what has made the church grow the last two thousand years.

Lord over the Universe or God of the Force?

Probably the most blatant and egregious error of Dr. Peck is his view of God. The god of Peck is but an idol invented by his mind. He combines his personal experience in Eastern religion with the teachings of liberal theologians such as Teilhard de Chardin, Paul Tillich and Erich Fromm.

The God of the Bible has revealed Himself to be a personal being who is above His creation and not a part of it. Yet He has chosen of His own free and sovereign will to enter into the universe of time-space-matter which He created to have a personal relationship with the people He has created. He has moved from transcendence (aboveness and apartness) to immanence (nearness) most fully by taking upon Himself the very nature of a creature in the person of Jesus Christ. Because of the incarnation, God is now and forever both transcendent and immanent.

God Is the Immanent One

Peck really only understands the immanence of God. In Peck's mind, God is not a separate, loving being, but an impersonal force little better than the force of Star Wars. Perhaps in his move to Christian theology Peck has not really put off the mantle of Buddhism, in which God and the world are identified.

As Peck develops his particular brand of eastern religion in combination with aspects of Christianity, he comes to identify God as being our unconsciousness. Our growth comes as we bring this unconscious god into our personal consciousness. In Peck's books, he seems at times to believe in a personal God who can communicate with us, a God who really loves us and cares for us. On the other hand he speaks of God in an eastern mystical way, being some underlying reality which can as easily be called "it" as He. This impersonal deity of Dr. Peck lacks the personal attributes of the God presented in the Bible who is not only inside of us but above and apart from us.

Peck's leanings toward Buddhism lead him to imply that God is really an abstraction, a view explained by Royce Gruenler:

> It must be remembered that principles do not do anything; persons do. Principles are merely abstractions that persons use to describe certain behavior, and must not be mistaken for the agent who is acting. Whitehead warned against committing "the fallacy of misplaced concreteness," and was himself eminently guilty of it when he ascribed personal activity and personal pronouns to the unconscious and impersonal primordial nature of God. Ford is also guilty of the fallacy when he reduces the Trinity to abstract principles, as in Cobb when he offers two sheer abstractions as ultimate. This simply will not do. It is illicit use of language drawn from actual persons acting as agents.[19]

Unlike the personal, ever present, but transcendent God of the biblical revelation, Peck's god is merely the combination of all the separate created entities in the universe. More particularly, God is the universal consciousness which we through spiritual growth can become. As Peck finally clarifies: "To put it plainly, our unconscious is God. God within us. We were part of God all the time,

God has been with us all along, is now, and always will be."[20]

God is immanent in His world, but Peck's use of the term is dangerous, for God is not simply near to His creation; He is His creation. Peck's view is heretical. God's nearness to, yet not identity with, creation and God's transcendence, apart from and above His creation, is the proper balance. This is the only way to avoid error.

God in Three Persons, Blessed Trinity

The familiar hymn, "Holy, Holy, Holy," speaks of the nature of God, especially as it relates to God's Trinity, three persons in one. Dr. Peck speaks of God often and Jesus often; I don't remember his ever placing these two persons within the purview of the ancient creeds of the church.[21]

This doctrine of the Trinity is abundantly clear in the teachings of the New Testament and implicit in the Hebrew Scriptures. The New Testament speaks of the Father, Son and Holy Spirit in doxologies as well as individual discussions of the three persons (for example, 2 Corinthians 13:14). Moreover, there is evidence of the Trinity at Jesus' baptism (Matthew 3:16-17), the great commission (Matthew 28:19) and the various talks to His disciples when He spoke of His relationship to the Father and to the Spirit (John 14, 16, 17).

You Too Can Become God

When the serpent made the statement that Adam and Eve could be as God, or gods, if they partook of the tree of the knowledge of good and evil, he offered something they should never have desired. God is the one who establishes what is good or evil. By hoping to take the position of God (see Genesis 3:22) they usurped the prerogative of deity to decide right and wrong. They assert their perspectives over against God's. This is also the temptation that Dr. Peck offers to those persons reading his books. He says his readers can become God.

210

He then posits the questions as to why God wants us to grow and toward what. Saying he doesn't want to involve himself in "theological niceties" or "speculative theology," he goes on:

> God wants us to become Himself (or Herself or Itself). We are growing toward godhood. God is the goal of evolution. It is God who is the source of the evolutionary force and God who is the destination. That is what we mean when we say that He is the Alpha and the Omega, the beginning and the end.[22]

This may be what Peck means, but this is not what Jesus meant in the Revelation of John. This is heresy and blasphemy!

Peck continues:

> It is one thing to believe in a nice old God who will take good care of us from a lofty position of power which we ourselves could never begin to attain. It is quite another to believe in a God who has it in mind for us precisely that we should attain His position, His power, His wisdom, His identity. . . . We don't want to have to work that hard. We don't want God's responsibility. . . . As long as we can believe that godhood is an impossible attainment for ourselves, we don't have to worry about our spiritual growth, we don't have to push ourselves to higher and higher levels of consciousness and loving activity; we can relax and just be human.[23]

Peck has totally misunderstood the nature of God and man. We are not going to become even close to the infinite, transcendent, immanent, all-powerful, knowing and present God of the biblical revelation. Peck's god is far, far less. He is a nonpersonal, finite something, not much more than humanity. We should not frustrate people or deceive them into reaching for the unattainable. The god envisioned by Peck is no more significant than the idols Israel crafted and bowed before (Isaiah 44:9ff).

And Peck has a response to those of us would reject his teaching on our achieving godhood: "It is no wonder that the belief in the possibility of Godhead is repugnant. . . . The idea that God is actively nurturing us so that we might grow up to be like Him brings us face to face with our own laziness."[24] But laziness is not the problem. The underlying root of sin is to exalt our will and perspective on good and evil above God's declaration.

Is God He, She or It?

Dr. Peck makes much of his personal idea of God and the sense of relation that he had with God. In *People of the Lie* he speaks of God in masculine terms.

> Many readers are likely to be concerned about my use of masculine pronouns in relation to God. I think I both understand and appreciate their concern. It is a matter to which I have given much thought. I have generally been a strong supporter of the women's movement and action that is reasonable to combat sexist language. But first of all, God is not neuter. He is exploding with life and love—even sexuality of a sort. So "It" is not appropriate. Certainly I consider God androgynous. He is as gentle and tender and nurturing and maternal as any woman could ever be. Nonetheless, culturally determined though it may be, I subjectively experience His reality as more masculine than feminine. While He nurtures us, He also desires

to penetrate us, and while we more often than
not flee from His love like a reluctant virgin, He
chases after us with a vigor in the hunt that we
most typically associate with males. As C.S. Lewis put it, in relation to God we are all female.[25]

Subsequently, Dr. Peck seems to have retreated. In his
later books he calls God He or She or It. Often he uses
He/She as designations (see the chart on page 75).

Though his new usage may be much more pleasing to
many politically correct people, especially radical feminists, I
need to emphasize that God is *not* a sexual being. God is not
male or female or androgynous, male *and* female. God is
spirit, while sexuality is inherent in the physical world. On
the other hand, masculinity and femininity are not strictly
physical in nature. There are personality traits generally associated with men and women, though some are held in
common. God is consistently portrayed in Scripture and in
nature, in agreement with C.S. Lewis' point above, as a masculine person, expressing essentially masculine personality
traits. This does not preclude that certain feminine traits are
also expressed by God. The Old Testament speaks of God
metaphorically like a hen concerned with her chicks. Apart
from figures, however, the God of Israel is depicted as a masculine person, the husband, whereas the nations around Israel had both gods and goddesses.

The person of God the Father and Jesus the Son is an
eternal relationship. When Christ came into the world as a
male being, His personhood was not neuter but masculine
and so naturally occupied a male physical body.

God made Adam and Eve after His image (Genesis 2:21-
23). The image of God was not restricted to masculine personhood but certain traits which could be expressed in the
male/masculine Adam and the female/feminine Eve. God
the Father, however, tends toward this masculinity in His
relation toward God the Son for all eternity, and in time toward His creation.

The Ever-Changing God in Peck's Theology

Scripture and the church fathers present God as the un-changing one. He is constant in His power, knowledge and being, so that He becomes the static but stable being who can always be relied on to be in control and ever just in His relations with humanity. This perspective of God is advanced in both the Old and New Testaments (Malachi 3:6; John 3:27; James 1:16).

Peck has adopted a theology of God known as process theism.[26] In this view God is constantly evolving into a higher being. Rather than being all-powerful and all-knowing, He is still learning and is not capable of doing everything. He is within the machine of the world and is in some respect controlled by it as we are, and is heading, and leading us, toward an uncertain future.

Peck speaks favorably of this type of changing and limited god:

> And we think God is as God was and will always be. But it's not the way I think anymore. And increasingly it's not what the theologians are beginning to think. Thank God! If there is anything that characterizes life, it is change. As already mentioned, what most distinguishes the animate from the inanimate is irritability. Something that's animate moves when you poke at it. It doesn't just sit there. It's alive. It goes this way and that way. It grows, it decays, it gets reborn. It changes. All life is in process. And since I choose to have a living God, I believe that my God is in process, learning and growing and perhaps even laughing and dancing.[27]

Peck has chosen to have the kind of god he wants. He has created a finite god to worship, a god in his own image. His conception of any form of life is change, decay and rebirth, so God is supposed to behave that way. Surely the created order reacts this way, but *not* the God who creates, the Uncaused and Unchanging One.

Who Is the Jesus of M. Scott Peck?

Jesus Christ is the focus of Christianity. In other religions of the world, the moral teachings of the religion serve to provide the essence of the religion. Buddhism would continue if Buddha never lived. Islam could still have a vital belief in Allah even if another than Mohammed were not his prophet. This is not true of Christianity. It is doubtful that Christianity would have survived the persecutions of the early Christian centuries or blossomed to its magnitude today apart from the belief in the special nature and work of Jesus Christ. Jesus is not merely appreciated for His teachings or respected for His high moral standings. He is worshiped, adored and obeyed as the sovereign God and creator of the universe, the Savior of His people. Peck's teaching uses Christian terminology at times but his Christ has little resemblance to the Jesus Christ of history and faith. For Peck, Jesus is little more, if any more, than other founders of religion. Not only is He an average religious leader, He is a troubled and frustrated person who was rude to people and confused about His role as Savior. Let us explore the Jesus of M. Scott Peck.

"Jesus was an example of the Western mystic," says Dr. Peck.[28] He never really explains what he means by such a term but since Peck develops much of his views of God and reality from Eastern mysticism, it is reasonable to assume he is using the word in this sense. Eastern mystics are those who have disciplined themselves to experience reality is such a way that they become one with the universe. They fuse their identity and consciousness with the world. They become one with God.[29] This seems to be what Peck means, for he says:

He integrated himself with God: "I am in the Father and the Father in me." He blurred the distinction between himself and others: "Inasmuch as you have done it unto the least of these . . . ye have done it unto me." . . . Finally, He gave . . . the proper paradoxical attitude toward self when He proclaimed, "Whosoever will save his life [self] will lose it, and whosoever will lose his life [self] for my sake [i.e., in the right way] will find it."[30]

The implication of Peck's view is that though Jesus was a mystic, He only stands alongside other famous mystics such as Buddha, Krishna, Confucius, and Mohammed.

To believe that Jesus is one among other religious teachers—even to be the best one—is a distortion of biblical truth and demeaning to Jesus. Peter told Jesus, "You are the Christ, the Son of the living God" (Matthew 16:16). Jesus indicated to Peter that he knew this truth because of divine revelation by the Father.

For eternal salvation a person must recognize Jesus for the exalted being He is. In speaking to the religious leaders of Israel, Jesus exclaimed, "Unless you believe that I am . . . you shall die in your sins" (John 8:24). On another occasion He told the leaders, "Before Abraham was, I AM" (John 8:58). They did not miss His pronouncement of being the God of Abraham, Isaac and Jacob, the eternal I AM, Creator of the universe and His people Israel (Exodus 3:14). To claim anything less for Jesus is to treat Him with contempt and to reject the forgiveness He offers.

Jesus in the Image of Peck

The Jesus seen by Peck "between the lines" of the New Testament text is a figment in the mind of Dr. Peck, not the Jesus portrayed in the Gospels and believed in the church.

We have already discovered the biblical Christ in the

216

foregoing portion of text. In reading the New Testament accounts of Christ's life in the Gospels and then observing the faith of the church toward their resurrected Lord, I do not see the Jesus Peck sees. Rather, Peck has created a Jesus who reflects his own inadequate searching for spiritual health.

Peck's Evaluation of Jesus

Dr. Peck discovers in Jesus a troubled man, usually frustrated, not very happy.

> I discovered a man who was almost continually frustrated. His frustration leaps out of virtually every page: "What do I have to say to you? How many times do I have to say it? What do I have to do to get through to you?" I also discovered a man who was frequently sad and sometimes depressed, frequently anxious and scared. A man who was prejudiced on one occasion, although He was able to overcome that prejudice and transcend it in healing love. A man who was terribly, terribly lonely, yet often desperately needed to be alone. I discovered a man so incredibly real that no one could have made Him up.[31]

To Peck, Jesus was sexually interested in people whom he associated with. Peck intimates that Jesus had sexual relations with Mary Magdalene, a prostitute, and John, the disciple "whom Jesus loved." Peck could only intimate this because he accepts both extramarital and homosexual relationships as healthy.[32] There is not one shred of biblical evidence that Jesus was involved sexually with anyone.

Unlike the person presented by Peck, Jesus was in total control of Himself, His emotions, actions and destiny. He is the perfect example of balance. He was calm in the midst of a storm on Galilee, transferring His own inner calm to the sea around Him. He could take the toughest questioning and not become flustered or want for an answer. He mixed gentleness with tough love. He knew when to turn aside to rest and when to press on in His work. He controlled even the timing of His betrayal. There has never been anyone remotely close to Jesus Christ in simplicity, erudition, humility, certitude, compassion and sacrifice. He is the Creator God who entered into His creation to suffer as a Man with the worth of God.

Jesus, God and Man

The various church councils between A.D. 325 and 451 sought to come to grips with the Person of Jesus Christ. Did He truly share the same essence as the Father? Was He fully God? The last council, Chalcedon (A.D. 451), established a balance between the humanity and deity of Christ. The churchmen knew this was biblical truth, but they were not able to determine exactly how He could be fully God and fully Man in one Person.

M. Scott Peck seems to adopt the Chalcedonian creed of Jesus being both God and man in his book *Further Along the Road Less Traveled*. He speaks against the extremes of viewing either the full humanity or full deity of Jesus as nothing more than an appearance. When I read these statements by Peck toward the end of *Further Along the Road Less Traveled*, my first thought was that maybe he really has made some significant progress toward biblical faith.[33] In reflection, though, I remembered the many times he had invested his words with different meanings than normally understood.

Since Dr. Peck still believes that God is not a separate entity from His connection with us, a pantheistic view, his statements may mean no more than that the man Jesus had gained the ability to cause His conscious mind to tap directly into His unconscious. On the other hand, Peck may be coming to understand that Jesus is the preexistent God of the Bible and the creeds. Perhaps he is beginning to realize that Jesus came to take on Himself humanity while retaining His deity. If so, Peck could be making significant progress toward biblical faith.

The Savior Who Helps Those Who Help Themselves

When Dr. Peck was being interviewed by Ben Patterson for *Christianity Today,* he was asked what he meant when he called Christ Savior. Peck's answer reveals that he has little understanding of the New Testament teaching on the subject.

He said that there are three different ways in which this could be understood. The least favorite view to him is a Savior who atones for our sins. The second is to view Jesus as a kind of fairy godmother who rescues us when we get into trouble. The third is to see Jesus as one who shows us the way to salvation through the example of His life and death. He reiterates this definition when he says elsewhere, "Becoming the most we can be is also the definition of salvation."[34]

The concept of salvation clearly presented in the New Testament and the history of the church is the view he finds most unacceptable. He believes it compromises human responsibility. We would be tempted to live our lives passively in the face of sin and evil.[35]

What Peck Thinks About the Afterlife

Heaven Yes, but Hell No

Peck admits that while he considers reincarnation to be a possible truth, he really prefers the idea of heaven to this now.[36] He says:

> While open to the possibility of reincarnation, I perhaps would be more passionate about it were there not an alternative way of dealing with the issue, which has come to appeal to me much

more deeply—namely, the traditional Christian belief in life after death with its concepts of Heaven, Hell, and Purgatory. Although Purgatory is primarily a Roman Catholic notion, the psychiatrist in me takes to it with ease. I imagine Purgatory as a very elegant, well-appointed psychiatric hospital with the most modern and highly developed techniques for making learning as gentle and painless as possible under divine supervision.[37]

Notice that Dr. Peck does not present any arguments for belief in reincarnation, heaven or purgatory and no evidence that hell doesn't exist. It is all a matter of preference or feeling. This is a characteristic trait of how he develops theology. Moreover, even the purgatory that he accepts is far different than the view as taught in the Roman Catholic Church.

Peck accepts heaven and purgatory but rejects the biblical teaching on hell.[38] Not only this, he rejects the biblical teaching of resurrection, a cornerstone of the Christian faith.

The Importance of the Resurrection

The resurrection of our bodies, in the teaching of the New Testament, is the culmination of our salvation (see Romans 8; 1 Thessalonians 4; 1 Corinthians 1). Unlike the Greek view of the body and spirit, in which the body merely dissolved but the spirit continued on, both Hebrew and Christian Scriptures set forth the physical, fleshly resurrection of the body in the last days. Paul goes so far to argue that if there is no fleshly resurrection then Jesus Himself did not rise from the dead, putting the very forgiveness of our sins in doubt (1 Corinthians 15:1-34).

What about the biblical teaching on resurrection of the body? Contrary to the teaching of the historic Christian church, Dr. Peck says that he finds "distasteful the traditional idea of Christianity which preaches the resurrection of the body."[39] He then provides the reason why he rejects this foundational biblical teaching. It is not because he is convinced by certain biblical texts of its wrongness, or because it is somehow contrary to logic. No, it is for purely pragmatic reasons:

> Frankly, I see my body as more of a limitation than a virtue, and I will be glad to be free of it rather than having to continue to cart it around. I prefer to believe that souls can exist independently from bodies. I think it is possible for souls to exist independently of bodies and even to be developed independently of bodies. Certainly all the literature describing near-death experiences tends to support this view.[40]

Peck is correct that spirits can live independently of bodies but we will forever live after the resurrection in a time-space-matter universe and will need our bodies to function effectively and completely in that existence. We are finite and will always be limited in capabilities. The resurrection body, however, will not be subject to death or decay (1 Corinthians 15:35-49). As far as near-death experiences being a proof for his view, see the detailed studies by Richard Abanes.[41]

What Is Peck's Problem?

M. Scott Peck is not an unintelligent man. He is not even a religiously disinterested person. Why, then, is he so very wrong about so much within the Christian faith that he claims to embrace? Why is he so far off base in his perception of the God and Jesus whom he claims to love? The reason for his failure to come to the truth may be explained in the words of Gruenler and Polanyi:

> With Polanyi I would agree that Christian faith discloses itself only to the attentive and obedi-

ent disciple who approaches it in heuristic expectation. In other words, Christian theology can be done authentically only by believing Christians in a setting of Christian "conviviality." . . . In the final analysis it is apprenticeship within the worshipping community that affords the apprentice, journeyman, and master himself (or herself) the proper context for interpreting Christian theology with fidelity to its biblical origins and historic past; otherwise the locus of authority will simply shift from the authority of the Scriptures to the authority of the secular interpreter. As Polanyi says, "Only a Christian who stands in the service of his faith can understand Christian theology and only he can enter into the religious meaning of the Bible."[42]

Endnotes

1. Peck, M. Scott. *Further Along the Road Less Traveled* (New York: Simon and Schuster, 1993), p. 159.

2. Peck, *Further,* p. 200.

3. Peck, *Further,* p. 107.

4. Peck, *Further,* p. 107.

5. Peck, *Further,* p. 107.

6. Peck, *Further,* p. 107.

7. The writers of Hebrew Scripture view God's deliverance from Egypt by God's miraculous hand and His creation of the world as true history. Christ and the apostles speak of persons such as Adam, Abraham, David, Jonah as real people and events such as creation, the destruction of Sodom and the Exodus as real historical events.

8. For evidence of the veracity and inerrancy of Scripture, see Clark Pinnock, *Biblical Revelation* (Chicago: Moody Press, 1971); Edward J. Young, *Thy Word Is Truth* (Grand Rapids: Wm. B. Eerdmans Publishing Company, 1957, 1976).

9. Peck, *Further,* p. 107.

10. Peck, *Further,* p. 107.

11. See the excellent studies on biblical interpretation and understanding of literary forms in Berkeley Mickelson, *Interpreting the Bible* (Grand Rapids: Baker Book House, 1994); Leland Ryken, *Words of Delight: A Literary Introduction to the Bible* (Grand Rapids: Baker Book House, 1987); Gordon D. Fee and Douglas Stuart, *How to Read the Bible for All Its Worth: A Guide to Understanding the Bible* (Grand Rapids: Zondervan Publishing House, 1982).

12. Peck, *Further,* p. 80.

13. Peck, *Further,* p. 113.

14. Peck, *Further,* pp. 113-114.

15. n.a. "Scott Peck Speaks Out about the Church, Community, and Crystals," *The Door* (May-June 1990), p. 10.

16. Peck, *Further,* p. 200.

17. n.a. *The Door,* p. 14.

18. Peck, *Further,* p. 166.

19. Gruenler, Royce Gordon. *The Inexhaustible God* (Grand Rapids: Baker Book House, 1983), pp. 62-63.

20. Peck, M. Scott. *The Road Less Traveled* (New York: Simon and Schuster, 1978), p. 281.

21. I am thinking primarily of the ancient creeds: the Apostles' Creed, the Nicene Creed and the Athanasian Creed.

22. Peck, *The Road,* p. 270.

23. Peck, *The Road,* p. 270.

24. Peck, *The Road,* p. 271.

25. Peck, M. Scott. *People of the Lie* (New York: Simon and Schuster, 1983), p. 12. Lewis quote is from *That Hideous Strength* (New York: Macmillan, 1965), p. 316.

26. Peck, M. Scott. *A World Waiting to Be Born* (New York: Simon and Schuster, 1993), p. 360.

27. Peck, *A World,* p. 361.

28. Peck, *A World,* p. 21.

29. Elwell, Walter A., ed. *Evangelical Dictionary of Theology* (GrandRapids: Baker Book House, 1984), p. 744.

30. Peck, *A World,* p. 21.

31. Peck, *Further,* p. 160.

32. Peck, *A World,* p. 77; Peck, *Further Along the Less Traveled Road,* p. 104.

33. Peck, *Further,* p. 206.

34. Peck, *A World,* p. 12.

35. Patterson, Ben. "Is God a Psychotherapist?" *Christianity Today* (March 1, 1985): 21.

36. Peck, *Further,* p. 169.

37. Peck, *Further,* p. 169.

38. Peck, *Further,* p. 171.

39. Peck, *Further,* pp. 168-169.

40. Peck, *Further,* p. 169.

41. Abanes, Richard. *Embraced By The Light and the Bible* (Camp Hill, PA: Christian Publications, 1994).

42. Polanyi, Michael. *Personal Knowledge: Towards a Post-Critical Philosophy* (New York: Harper & Row, 1964) as quoted in Gruenler, p. 144.

CHAPTER 10

Further Along the Wrong Road: Spirituality without Morality

. . . [I]n order to love God passionately, one has to be a passionate, sexual person.

—M. Scott Peck[1]

Shocking as it may seem, I think there is a genuine sexual element in the relationship between human beings and God. What this means, if I am correct, is not only that we human beings are sexual creatures, but also that God is in fact a sexual being.

—M. Scott Peck[2]

It's very important you readers realize that I am a phony and a hypocrite.

M. Scott Peck[3]

M. Scott Peck must consider himself to be an authority on the Bible, for he devotes much of his writing toward explaining what he believes to be "traditional Christian" viewpoints. But are Peck's characterizations of biblical doctrine correct? Hardly! From what Peck has written, it is obvious that he is not a Bible scholar, nor even a knowledgeable Bible student. I see no problem with Peck expressing his opinions on any issue; it is important his readers understand, however, that most of the views espoused by Peck are in direct opposition to the truths presented in the Bible. Let us not be deceived; Peck does not teach Christianity.

I am not suggesting that Peck is unintelligent, insincere or harbors any bad intentions. Where Peck stands, as an individual before God, is not ultimately for others to decide. What we can and should focus on is the sentiments he inculcates and the concepts he promotes. To examine his beliefs in the light of the Scripture is our Christian duty, especially since he claims to speak from a Christian perspective.

Most of the second portion of this book has examined Peck's perspectives on questions of theology; I shall now briefly deal with issues of morality that Peck touches on in his writings. Here, too, I am disturbed by what I see in his books. He speaks of spirituality, but it is a spirituality without moral foundation.

The Apostle Paul tells us that we need to "[T]est everything. Hold on to the good" (1 Thessalonians 5:21). So let us place Peck on the couch and listen to what he has to say. We shall measure him with the Word of God; it will be our standard. Peck will rise or fall by his own words. We begin our investigation with Peck's concept of morality.

The Spiritual Nature of Sex

Dr. Peck speaks much of sexuality. This should not surprise us particularly. What is especially interesting is that he equates sexuality and spirituality. He believes that they are so closely related that the sexual urge actually rises out of our unconscious desire to reunite with the divine. It is, as he puts it, "an urge toward wholeness and a yearning for the godhead."[4] He is so convinced of the link that he comments, "Even atheists or agnostics, at the moment of orgasm, cry out, 'Oh, my God!' or, 'Oh Christ!' They may say, 'I don't believe in God,' but at the moment of ecstasy, or maybe at the moment of agony, they're yelling, 'Oh God!' "[5]

Peck's attempt to equate the use of God's name in the midst of sexual excitement as religious has little to commend it as a proof anymore than when an atheist or agnostic hits his thumb with a hammer and uses God's name. Peck is grabbing at straws here.

For Dr. Peck, the "sexual and the spiritual parts of our personality lie so close together that it is hardly possible to arouse one without arousing the other."[6] Such a view would seem to make our future existence in heaven, in our physical bodies, a difficult situation since there seem to be no sexual needs in heaven. In this regard we are like the angels since there is no need to propagate the race (Mark 12:25).

Surely, when a man and woman share each other in a sexual act, they may be expressing themselves to each other in more than physical terms, but hardly does this mean that somehow they are involved in a religious experience with each other or with God Himself.

Peck likes to make the point that many Christians are reticent to talk about sex, or that they believe it is a dirty subject. He is not presenting a completely accurate picture, however. The Bible considers sex a wonderful gift from God, but it is only proper between a man and a woman within the bounds of marriage. Adultery and fornication are evil in the eyes of God (see Romans 1:28-29; 1 Corinthians 6:9). Christians are instructed to honor God with their bodies and to abstain from sex outside of marriage (Hebrews 13:4).

Open Marriages

Marriage is not inviolate to Dr. Peck. He is very open to sexual relations outside of marriage and strongly rejects the idea that a couple should always maintain an exclusive commitment to one another:

> [T]he American or Western myth of romantic love suggests that certain people are "meant for each other"; thus, by extrapolation, they are not meant for anyone else. The myth, here, prescribes exclusivity for loving relationships, most particularly sexual exclusivity. . . . The first obligation of a genuinely loving person will always be to his or her marital and parental relationships. Nonetheless, there are some whose capacity to love is great enough for them to build loving relationships successfully within the family and still have energy left for additional relationships. For these the myth of exclusivity is not only patently false, but also represents an unnecessary limitation upon their capacity to give of themselves to others outside their family.[7]

In case the reader does not get the point of Peck's message—that extramarital affairs are acceptable—he further explains, "My work with couples has led me to the stark conclusion that open marriage is the only kind of mature marriage that is healthy and not seriously destructive to the spiritual health and growth of the individual partners."[8]

Though Peck does not speak in vivid terms of what he is advocating, in endorsing the book on "open marriage" by Nena and George O'Neill, there is little question on what he means (for a fuller explanation of their views, see the discussion of their book in Part 1). Suffice it to say that what Peck advocates as "open marriage" is a softened name for adultery. But the Bible constantly opposes adultery (Exodus 20:14; Deuteronomy 5:18; Matthew 19:18). When a man and woman unite together in marriage, it is intended that they shall be committed solely to one another, for they have become "one flesh" before God (Mark 10:7-8). The writer of Hebrews is quite blunt: "Marriage should be honored by all, and the marriage bed kept pure, for God will judge the adulterer and all the sexually immoral" (Hebrews 13:4). God is opposed to adultery (open marriage), and for this reason alone we should reject what Peck would ask us to embrace. In addition, however, it is safe to argue that extramarital affairs are destructive to the health and stability of the family. It can only be concluded that open marriage is damaging to both the spiritual and emotional bonds of marriage.

Sexuality and God

It is not surprising that Peck supports open marriage, for his ideas concerning sexuality are incompatible with the Bible's. For one thing, Peck believes that at the very climax of orgasm we forget who and where we are and for a brief moment we leave this earth and enter God's country.[9] To refute this statement is to give it some measure of credibility, when in fact, from a biblical standpoint it is nonsense, perhaps even delusional. Is the Christian God sexually interested in human beings? Peck seems to think so. He proposes that "there is a genuine sexual element in the relationship between human beings and God."[10] Furthermore, he describes the Song of Solomon as "an exquisite, erotic duet between God and His or Her people."[11] Where is Peck going with all these sexual connotations concerning God? It seems as if Peck is suggesting that God possesses a libido. This is no exaggeration, for Peck does believe that God is a sexual being.[12] He actually says that God is on the make.[13]

Scripture presents God as a spirit (John 4:24). Figurative expressions of God, such as His hand, arm, etc., are meant to express in human terms (anthropomorphisms) the fact that God sees, hears and acts. To my knowledge there is no example of God expressing a sexual impulse or having genitalia.[14]

The Sexual Attitudes and Actions of Christ

The Bible declares that God loved us so much that to save us from our impending destruction, He came to earth as the man Christ Jesus (John 1:1, 14). Jesus is in fact the second Person of the Holy Trinity. He Himself declared, "Anyone who has seen me has seen the Father" (John 14:9). It follows, therefore, that all the reader needs to do, to discover the true nature and personality of God, is to look at the attitudes and actions of Christ.

How does Peck see Christ? The same as he sees God—namely, Someone who is sexually interested in His people. In view of this, he strongly intimates that Jesus had sexual relations with Mary Magdalene and also with His disciple John. Peck declares that Jesus was an androgynous being. Speaking of this sexuality hidden in the Gospel records he asserts:

> Jesus' sense of humor, for instance, and His sexuality. The latter may have been left out on purpose because Jesus' sexuality seems to me rather ambiguous. He appears to have been very fond of Mary Magdalene, who might have been a prostitute, and He is frequently pictured in an intimate pose with the Apostle John, who is referred to as "the one whom Jesus loved." I believe that Jesus was an androgynous figure; that is, not without sex, or unisexed, but whole.[15]

Dr. Peck, apparently, doesn't believe that it is possible to have love for someone without wanting to have sex with him or her. His perverse perspective should not surprise us (as will be revealed in the section below on sex and psychotherapy), but he has struck a new low in charging the Lord Jesus with having sex with His followers.

We know that Jesus was without sin (Hebrews 4:15). He did not even look at women lustfully, for this would be adultery (Matthew 5:28). Though Christ loves us, and came to sacrifice Himself in our place, there is not even a hint of His having any sexual interest in anyone. Again it cannot be stressed enough, Christ did not sin (1 Peter 2:22). This means that Christ did not harbor lustful thoughts, He did not engage in fornication or homosexual acts. As I said above, God is spirit, and there is no indication whatsoever that He lusts after our bodies or has a sexual interest in us (John 4: 24).

Homosexuality Expresses God's Love of Variety

Of course Peck denies the fact that fornication and homosexuality are immoral and sinful acts against God. In some cases Peck even encourages his patients to engage in premarital sex.[16] And concerning homosexuality, Peck has this to say:

> But we cannot neglect the fact that God also calls us through our genes. . . . Sometimes it is the task of psychiatrists to assist homosexuals to come out of the closet in relation not only to others but also to themselves—to not only accept their calling to homosexuality but, insofar as possible, to rejoice in it. God loves variety; in variety he/she delights.[17]

God is utterly opposed to homosexuality. Genesis tells us that the people of Sodom and Gomorrah were homosexuals, and their sin so grieved the Lord that ultimately He destroyed them and their cities. The book of Jude indicates that this was the major sin of Sodom (Jude 7).

The creation accounts demonstrate that God's purpose is for men and women to unite, bear children and express joint stewardship (Genesis 1:26-28; 2:25). This happens in marriage; it can only perversely occur in a homosexual "union." Jesus reiterates this creation theme when He says, "But at the beginning of creation God 'made them male and female' " (Mark 10:6). This verse makes clear God's intention for man and woman to unite, but not man with man or woman with woman. Paul explains in Romans 1:27 that it is only natural for men to be sexually attracted to women, and vice versa, but it is unnatural for men to lust after men, or for women to desire other women. Homosexuality is a perversion (Leviticus 18:22; Romans 1:27; Jude 7) of God's intentions for His creation.

Sexual Relations with Clients

Peck considers sex a driving force to defining one's identity, developing spiritual growth and bringing about mental health. He admits that if it would work he would have sex with his patients:

> [W]ere I ever to have a case in which I concluded after careful and judicious consideration that my patient's spiritual growth would be substantially furthered by our having sexual relations, I would proceed to have them. In fifteen years of practice, however, I have not yet had such a case, and I find it difficult to imagine that such a case could really exist.[18]

Peck follows this shocking comment with rationale why a psychiatrist usually should not have sex with a patient. It relates to the fact that a therapist is primarily in the role of a good parent, who should not have sex with his or her children for two reasons. A parent is to be of use to a child and not a child of use to the parent, and the job of a parent is to lead the child toward independence and not dependence. Elsewhere Peck indicates that a child has a sexual attraction for a parent.[19]

232

Peck's arguments against incest sound specious. If therapists are not to use patients and parents are not to use children, but in an isolated case a therapist could have sex with his patient, then under this same logic parents could in isolated cases have sex with their children if it helped them. Peck, at one point, speaks approvingly of Joseph Fletcher's "situation" ethics. To Fletcher, the loving thing cannot be easily proscribed. Every situation is different and no rules can be established.[20] Peck's rationale does not hold. The only basis to avoid such problems is obedience to the absolute ethics of the Bible.

Peck Enjoys Pornography

In an interview with *Playboy,* Dr. Peck indicated that he enjoys looking at pornography and even considers it healthy.[21] This is not a statement like the interview with President Jimmy Carter, who admitted that he had adulterous thoughts. This is an admission of sin. In contrast, Peck's statements are approvingly made.

Peck must have skipped over those sections of the Bible which tell us to avoid sexual immorality (1 Thessalonians 4:3; 1 Corinthians 6:18) and lust (Matthew 5:28). We know that pornography is a major problem for our society, especially for men. Peck does no good to any of the men who read his writings by passing off this sinful impulse with a blessing.

Peck and Swearing

Peck has an interesting and partially accurate presentation on the matter of swearing. He claims that Christians' concerns about using foul language are an erroneous interpretation of the second commandment against taking God's name in vain.[22] To Peck, blasphemy is "using sweet religious language to cloak irreligious behavior." The violators of the second commandment are those who refuse "even to attempt to integrate behavior with theology."[23]

He calls this "the sin of sins" and uses an example of what he means by recounting a weekend he spent with a Christian couple in South Carolina:

> I spent a weekend with a born-again couple in South Carolina whose every other sentence was God did this and God did that, and God would do this and God would do that, interspersed with nasty gossip about who was sleeping with whom and who wasn't going to church and whose children had gone sour. When I finally got out of there after three days, I thought if I'd heard God did this and God did that one more time, I would have puked! Their sin was even graver to me than petty gossip because I felt all their "God talk" was blasphemous—the use of "the name of the Lord" in such a way as to trivialize God.[24]

While there is some truth in the statement that the second commandment has been misinterpreted to include "rough" language, there are other Scriptures commanding the believer to avoid filthy language (for example, Colossians 3:8).

Peck has no problem telling dirty jokes. He seems to have overlooked Paul's admonition: "[S]et an example for the believers in speech, in life, in love, in faith and in purity" (1 Timothy 4:12). Surely the use of language that either makes a mockery of the sexual relationship is a curse upon another individual or is an inappropriate use of the name of the Lord is not the example Jesus Christ gave us to follow.

Respect for Parents

Peck regularly blames his clients' problems on their parents. He portrays a good relationship with his parents but believes that children really should not have to obey their parents:

> Honor your father and mother that your days may be long upon the land. From the standpoint of psychiatry, it is probably the only thing in the entire Bible that needs rewriting. Radical rewriting. For the most part children naturally want to honor their parents.[25]

Peck makes much of the fact that Jesus supposedly did not like the idea of family.[26] Dr. Peck believes that allegiance to father and mother is a form of idolatry.

Not only does he believe this but in *The Road Less Traveled* he cites a personal instance. Contrary to his parents' wishes, when he was in high school, he refused to go back to the school they wanted for him to attend:

> First of all, the examples of the changes described and all other such major changes are acts of self-love. It is precisely because I valued myself that I was unwilling to remain miserable in a school and whole social environment that did not fit my needs. It is because the housewife had regard for herself that she refused to tolerate any longer a marriage that so totally limited her freedom and repressed her personality.[27]

Peck says that God does not work with organizations and units but with individuals.[28] This is true respecting individual salvation, but God places individuals in families and communities so they can learn about Him (Deuteronomy 6:4-9). One of the purposes of the church community is to help members live godly and circumspect lives in this world. Paul the apostle said that obedience to parents carries a promise—long life (Ephesians 6:2-3). Certainly people die who are obedient to parents, but by obeying parents we may avoid many things that bring premature death.

Addictions

There is little doubt based on Dr. Peck's own words, and the attestation by those who have talked with him, that he is addicted to at least cigarettes and possibly alcohol and drugs. He admits the former but fudges on the latter, seemingly in denial. His rationalizations do not excuse him from the biblical teaching on addiction. The abuse of alcohol, and, by implication, any addictive substance, is contrary to God's standards for us (Proverbs 20:1; 23:20-21; Ephesians 5:18; Titus 2:3). Those in leadership have an even higher standard (Titus 1:7).

Divorce

Occasionally I have had callers on my radio talk show tell me about counselors, usually non-Christians, who have encouraged them to divorce their spouses, since they may be a hindrance to the improvement of their mental health. Peck seems to follow many in his profession that desire to break up homes, contrary to the Word of God. He says, "Just because your marriage was wrong for you at fifty doesn't mean it wasn't right for you at thirty. Don't think it is possible for God to have called you into married life twenty-five years ago and now decide it is time to call you out of it?"[29] Elsewhere he says, "There is no question in my mind that God calls some people to divorce."[30]

I am not sure which God Peck is referring to who calls people to divorce as He calls them to marriage. The God of the Bible speaks of not dividing what He has put together (Genesis 2:24; Matthew 19:6), of hating divorce (Malachi 2:15-16), of forbidding divorce except in cases of adultery (Matthew 19:9) and desertion (1 Corinthians 7:15).

The foregoing examples of Dr. Peck's views on morality

are not intended to point him out as uniquely immoral. All of us have our failures, but the Christian response is to confess our sins to God, to correct our thinking in areas of failure and certainly not to advocate immoral actions as Peck has done. Such teaching is harmful for persons who are trying to make sense of their lives, to correct their lives. Dr. Peck's teaching on morality, as well as theology, will do nothing to alleviate these problems but will exacerbate them even more.

Endnotes

1. Peck, M. Scott. *Further Along the Road Less Traveled* (New York: Simon and Schuster, 1993), p. 223.

2. Peck, pp. 229-230.

3. "Scott Peck Speaks Out about the Church, Community, and Crystals," *The Door*, (May-June 1990), p. 14.

4. Peck, *Further*, p. 220.

5. Peck, *Further*, p. 220.

6. Peck, *Further*, p. 225.

7. Peck M. Scott. *The Road Less Traveled* (New York: Simon and Schuster, 1978), pp. 158-159.

8. Peck, *The Road*, p. 93

9. Peck, *Further*, p. 221.

10. Peck, *Further*, p. 229.

11 Peck, *Further*, p. 219.

12. Peck, *Further*, p. 230.

13. Peck, *Further*, p. 230.

14. One might want to use the Song of Solomon to indicate this. The Song should be understood as the love of a husband for his wife, but even if God is seen in the Song, His love for His people is illustrated as the deep love a husband has for his wife, not actual, literal sexual impulses that God has for individuals.

15. Peck, *Further*, p. 161.

16. Peck, *The Road*, p. 147.

17. Peck, M. Scott. *A World Waiting to Be Born* (New York: Simon and Schuster, 1993), p. 77.

18. Peck, *The Road*, p. 175-176.

19. Peck, M. Scott. *People of the Lie* (New York: Simon and Schuster, 1983), p. 155.

20. Peck, *The Road,* p. 159.

21. Sheff, David. "Playboy Interview: M. Scott Peck," *Playboy* (March 1992), p. 56.

22. Peck, *Further,* p. 210.

23. Peck, *Further,* p. 211.

24. Peck, *Further,* p. 211.

25. Peck, *A World,* p. 175.

26. Peck, *A World,* pp. 174-175.

27. Peck, *The Road,* pp. 134-136, 138.

28. Peck, *A World,* p. 174.

29. Peck, *A World,* p. 71.

30. Peck, *A World,* p. 111.

CHAPTER 11

The End of the Road: Dr. Peck's View of Final Salvation

Dr. Peck gives powerful new reasons for hope and confidence in our personal ability to change ourselves and our world.

—Vice-President Al Gore[1]

And God placed all things under his [Christ's] feet and appointed him to be head over everything for the church.

Ephesians 1:22

One of Dr. Peck's all-encompassing beliefs is that what the world needs now is "community" (a group of people who have made a commitment to learn to communicate with each other with increasing depth, authenticity, honesty and vulnerability).[2] He believes that this community must be focused on a commitment to learn to communicate with each other with increasing depth, authenticity, honesty and vulnerability. He believes that this community is absolutely essential to the well being and indeed the final survival of the human race. Furthermore, all that is required is a group of approximately 50 people willing to undergo his training. The cost of "two facilitators" or group leaders from his organization will be $1,500 a day, each, plus expenses.[3] Lack of money will deprive the vast majority of the world of participation in this greatest of all achievements.

Creating Community

If, as Dr. Peck says, we too want "the world to be saved," and if this "cannot" be done "without undergoing some kind of spiritual healing," where is the best place to look for solutions? Is it with Dr. Peck, a man who claims to be a Christian, yet who does not believe what Jesus said of Himself? Is his community the place to seek after truth that God has provided for us over the last four millennia? Dr. Peck claims to offer the solutions: "Demanding rules must both be learned and followed. But there are rules! Quite clear ones. Saving ones. They are not obscure. The purpose of this book [*The Different Drum*] is to teach these rules and encourage you to follow them. . . . For that is how the world will be saved."[4]

We as Christians do not accept this. As Christians, we get our knowledge from God through the Bible. Yet how do we know what we believe is right and what Peck believes is wrong? Many groups claim to have the truth. But truth is not left up to the individual. Truth is external to us. Truth is true whether I think it is or not. The Bible claims to be the Word of God. Jesus said to the Father, "[Y]our word is truth" (John 17:17; see also Ephesians 1:13, 4:15, 4:21). The New Testament as well as the Old Testament is "inspired by God, and profitable for teaching, for reproof, for correction, and for training in righteousness; that the man of God may be adequate, equipped for every good work" (2 Timothy 3:16-17). Thus the Bible is where we go in order to test the truth claim of any individual or group or denomination. "How can a young man keep his way pure? By living according to your word" (Psalm 119:9). Thus we have this basic, fundamental understanding of where to go for reliable knowledge to test "truth claims" such as those we find in Dr. Peck's books. Peck's teachings are not always internally consistent. Furthermore, they routinely contradict clear doctrines of the Scriptures. Dr. Peck's foundation for thought does not lie in historic, orthodox, biblical Christianity. The tower of books that he builds upon his foundation—his theology—is a tower of babble.

It is interesting to note that Dr. Peck has listed six "tools" that he utilizes in creating and building "Community." He states that he has taken methods from diverse sources: Christian monasticism, Quaker meetings, Alcoholics Anonymous and the Twelve Step Programs, group psychotherapy and the work of management consultants.[5] Of these sources, Christian monasticism, Quaker meetings, Alcoholics Anonymous and the Twelve Step Programs all had their formation and foundations within the Christian church. In addition, group psychotherapy and counseling not only have been practiced within the Christian church, but are required by God (see Proverbs 11:14, Numbers 27:21, Leviticus 26:40, Psalm 32:5, James 5:16, et al.). Finally business management was attempted from the beginning as well. For example, when Moses and the people left Egypt, Moses had too much work to manage alone. Therefore Moses' father-in-law counseled Moses to divide up the labor into manageable units, and to place proper leaders at the head of each unit (see Exodus 18:13-23). In the New Testament, when the work of the new Christian church became too great for the apostles to care for, they selected "seven men of good reputation, full of the Spirit and wisdom," whom they charged with caring for the temporal needs of the people (see Acts 6:1-7). In short, every principle that Peck uses to set up the guidelines for his "communities" has been derived from practices that have been established for thousands of years! It is a pity that Dr. Peck is unable to recognize this simple fact.

Historically and even today, the church has continually strived to reproduce and maintain itself. Unfortunately, Dr. Peck cannot see or acknowledge this fact. Peck cannot see that there is one Father, God, and one Son, Jesus Christ, who is Head over the church. Not every one of the children of God who make up the church are walking in absolute perfection of harmony with the Spirit. Although the body of Christ is perfect in its conception, it is marred by the sinful nature of humanity that continually disrupts even the most holy of institutions. Does this mean that the church is irrelevant, or even worse, a waste of time and energy? Not at all. The church, for all of its human frailty, has worked to provide for hundreds of millions of people the world over, and that generally without cost to the recipients.

Historically, the church has preached repentance and the gospel—the bad news and the good news. This proclamation has brought freedom to believers, a freedom from having to live up to an impossible standard. Dr. Peck would change this.

Dr. Peck's concept of "community" is a group that has made a commitment. Commitment "transcends" differences, enables effective communication. And, of course, effective communication eventually results in world peace. *But the rules to be "committed" to are numerous and heavy.*

Contrast this with what Jesus said in regard to living in the kingdom of God: "My yoke is easy and my burden is light" (Matthew 11:30). The choice is clear. We have Peck's path of spiritual development. Read his writings and you will see it is a path of legalism. You will sense the weight of his millstones. Christ, in contrast to Peck, sets us free from the law of sin and death. The best thing a person can do after a heavy dose of legalism is to read—and reread—Romans and Galatians. The truth in God's Word will set that person free.

Another problem prevalent throughout Dr. Peck's writings, but especially evident in *A Different Drum,* is his thesis that a community "which includes all faiths" is "the cure for the core of our greatest contemporary trouble."[6] It is a thesis built contrary to all scriptural injunctions and attestations: "You shall have no other gods before me" (Exodus 20:3). Dr. Peck believes that we do not need "Christian spiritual healing."[7] Rather, "the solution lies in the opposite direction: in learning how to appreciate—even celebrate—individual, cultural and religious differences and how to live with reconciliation in a pluralistic world."[7] This runs counter to Jesus' declaration, "I am the way and the truth and the life. No one comes to the Father except through me" (John 14:6). It runs counter to Jesus' instructions to make disciples, "teaching them to obey everything I have commanded you" (Matthew 28:19-20). Even Peck states, "We must be totally dedicated to truth. . . . [W]e must always hold truth."[9]

It may surprise some that Protestant, Catholic and Eastern Orthodox Christians all agree on the basic tenants of Christianity, the essentials of the Christian faith: That there is one God in three persons, Father, Son and Holy Spirit; in the incarnation of Jesus—God became flesh and dwelt among us, fully God and fully man; that the Bible is the Word of God; in the substitutionary death of Christ on the cross for us; that Christ is returning for us; and there is a final judgment awaiting those who do not trust in Christ for their salvation. We who know personally Christ the Creator, Christ the Savior and Redeemer look forward eagerly to His second coming. We have hope and assurance.

Spiritual Growth or Spiritual Death?

Dr. Peck dedicates the majority of the last half of his book to what he calls the four "stages of spiritual growth."[10] His stages should be compared and contrasted with a "Christian" spiritual life. Those that followed Christ during His earthly ministry were labeled "Christians." So even today, those who follow Jesus Christ as their Lord and Savior are correctly termed Christians (see chapter 1 for Dr. Peck's full definition).

These four states, or stages, identified by Peck, represent

different levels of potential personal growth. A person may grow rapidly through the stages until he or she reaches level four, or he or she may stagnate at a given level for his or her entire life, never quite realizing that there is more available to him or her at the next state.

Stage One

As proclaimed by Peck, stage one is filled with people trapped in "absent spirituality."[11] They have no need for any type of religious teachings. He terms this the "chaotic/anti-social"[12] stage. It contains nearly all young children and perhaps one in five adults who are spiritually underdeveloped "people of the lie." Regarding children, Peck seems to forget that Jesus encouraged His followers to "[l]et the little children come to me, and do not hinder them, for the kingdom of heaven belongs to such as these" (Matthew 19:14). How can those who comprise the kingdom of heaven be absent spiritually? Can it be Peck who is chaotic in his biblical understanding and antisocial toward those whom Jesus Himself associated with?

Stage Two

Dr. Peck relegates the Christian church to his "formal/institutional"[13] stage two. This is where one's vision of God "is almost entirely that of an external being."[14] Dr. Peck condemns those in "the church" for being not much different from those who live as incarcerated criminals in prison, who are "dependent upon an institution for their governance."[15] Peck's level two persons seem to be mindless automatons who cannot live apart from authority. This is *not* the biblical picture of the person living in Christ.

Dr. Peck fails to realize that no one is absolutely free. He or she is either a slave of sin or a slave of righteousness. Consider the following:

> You have been set free from sin and have become slaves to righteousness. I put this in hu-

man terms because you are weak in your natural selves. Just as you used to offer the parts of your body in slavery to impurity and to ever-increasing wickedness, so now offer them in slavery to righteousness leading to holiness. (Romans 6:18-19)

Slavery to righteousness is a glorious bondage!

Stage Three

Stage three people are the skeptics. Those who "no longer need to depend on an institution for their governance."[16] These have passed beyond the need for a church and its "silly myths."[17]

Dr. Peck considers these people to be the "truth seekers."[18] Yet he has provided no absolute standard for truth. A person wishing to build a house will buy high quality measuring tools in order to lay a precise and accurate foundation. It appears so far that Dr. Peck himself has passed over the third stage in arriving at the fourth. He has as yet provided no foundation for his premises regarding truth. Rather, he has simply imparted philosophies and concepts from many sources and done as he saw fit. Consider the people in the time of the Old Testament Judges and the results of their lives as they chose to live "as they saw fit." What Dr. Peck claims as biblical truths are nothing more than brute ignorance and misunderstandings of what the Bible clearly teaches.

Stage Four

This, the most mature of all stages, is where Dr. Peck is. He considers it to be a mystical/communal state, the endpoint of spiritual evolution where, if we are fortunate, we will possibly catch a glimpse of him as he walks manfully ahead of us leading the world to salvation (at $1,500 plus expenses). He seems to see himself as reigning like another god. He does not intend to belittle the rest of us who have finally attained his final level of "truth," which has thus far been based on theories and feelings that were derived from sources that remain anonymous. This fourth stage is in essence nothing more than a monistic, pantheistic view of the world as we should all see it.

All is one, and one is all. I'm god, you're god. The only problem with Peck's view is that again, it goes against everything that the Bible and the Christian church have taught. Peck still proclaims that this is but one of the many ways to God. The Bible teaches that only one road leads to heaven and eternal salvation. Christ is not some other "mystic" of the ages, as Peck contends. Jesus declares, "I am the way and the truth and the life. No one comes to the Father except through me" (John 14:6).

Concluding Remarks

Reading M. Scott Peck's books, one discovers a man who is on a journey. Dr. Peck is constantly seeking after new ideas and hoping to uncover new ways to know what he conceives as truth. I do not want to cast doubt on the sincerity of his search. Especially in his most recent book he develops additional thoughts on a variety of subjects which seem to indicate that he has altered some of his thinking. Some ideas look like orthodox Christian thinking, but I am very hesitant to accept them as such at present since his underlying views of the world, sin, grace and God appear to remain in error. For example, when he says he believes that Jesus is fully God and fully man, he sounds orthodox. But since he views God as impersonal and the unconscious self trying to get through to the conscious self, probably he views Jesus as merely someone who has reached stage four of his spiritual growth categories and thus has reached godhood.

If Peck wants to be a Christian in deed and thought, and not merely in word, he needs to renounce his Eastern mysticism and religious perspectives on God, humanity and reality. He needs to submit himself to the authority of the Bible, accepting its errorless status and interpreting it according to its plain and obvious sense. Last, he needs to receive Jesus as his substitution for his sins, recognizing that he is incapable of contributing to his own salvation.

Peck is on a thousand mile walk. Only one road leads to God and there are many side roads, road blocks and detours. He is going in the right general direction but he may miss the city of God with its narrow path unless he relies on the only detailed road map that God has given us: the Bible. At times I see some progress in him, but also many failures. I wish him best!

Endnotes

1. Peck, M. Scott. *A World Waiting to Be Born* (New York: Bantam, 1993), back cover endorsement.

2. n.a. "The Small Group Letter: Scott Peck Talks About Our Barriers to Community and Intimacy in the Church," *Discipleship Journal* (July-August 1988), p. 41.

3. n.a., *Community Described* (FCE promotional literature), n.d., p. 1.

4. Peck, M. Scott. *The Different Drum*, (New York: Simon & Schuster, 1987), p. 21.

5. Peck, *A World*, p. 277.

6. Peck, *The Different Drum*, p. 20.

7. Peck, *The Different Drum*, pp. 19-20.

8. Peck, *The Different Drum*, pp. 19-20.

9. Peck, *The Road Less Traveled* (New York: Simon & Schuster, 1978), p. 50

10. Peck, M. Scott. *Further Along the Road Less Traveled* (New York: Simon and Schuster, 1993), p. 119.

11. Peck, *Further*, p. 121.

12. Peck, *Further*, p. 121.

13. Peck, *Further*, pp. 122-123.

14. Peck, *Further*, p. 123.

15. Peck, *Further*, p. 122.

16. Peck, *Further*, p. 124.

17. Peck, *Further*, p. 124.

18. Peck, *Further*, p. 124.

Acknowledgements

We would like to thank the following persons for various forms of assistance in the production of this book:

**Rich Elliot
Richard Featherstone
Steven Jones
Gretchen Passantino
and
Paula Popejoy.**